Learn More Earn More

How self-development at work can boost your career prospects and income

Steve Wiseman

Learn More Earn More
by Steve Wiseman

Lawpack Publishing Limited
76–89 Alscot Road
London SE1 3AW

www.lawpack.co.uk

ISBN: 978-1-905261-65-9

Exclusion of Liability and Disclaimer

Contents

iii

About the author

Steve Wiseman is Chief Executive Officer at the Norwich and District Citizens Advice Bureau – a charity that provides free advice and assistance on legal rights and entitlements. This is his seventh consumer publication. His previous titles include *Leaves on the Line! How to Complain Effectively*, *Put it in Writing* and *Claim your Cash!* He has an MA in Education and Professional Development at the University of East Anglia and he has also worked as a civil servant, a lecturer and as a journalist.

Acknowledgements

A number of people have greatly helped me by reading through early drafts and being involved in informal discussions on aspects of the subject matter. Sincere thanks are due to them. Special mention should be made of Lorraine Earl, whose suggestions led to constructive improvements to the manuscript, and Jackie Saville, with whom I wrote the inspiration behind this book, *Managing Training and Development – A Resource Manual*, for Citizens Advice, the National Association of Citizens Advice Bureaux.

Introduction

About this book

Are you at a crossroads in life? Do you want to change your job or move on, but you are not sure in what direction you want to go? Perhaps you are scared of change? This book is here to help you take stock of your life so that you can consider how you can improve yourself by learning new skills.

You may be looking for a new vocation, or you may want to develop in the job you have now and improve your prospects. Maybe you are stuck in a rut and the only way you can advance yourself is by developing your skills. Perhaps you have a job you really enjoy and you just want to be able to do it better. Are you struggling, stressed out and demoralised because you are not getting a chance to shine? This book tells you how you can use your job as a platform for success, even if your employer is not being very co-operative on the training front.

DID YOU KNOW?

Learning brings more happiness than having sex, playing or watching sport, or doing the National Lottery (*Finding Happiness, Gallup/North Yorkshire TEC, 1997*).

95 per cent of us think that learning new things boosts our confidence (*National Adult Learning Survey, DfEE, 1998*).

92 per cent of us think that learning new things is enjoyable (*National Adult Learning Survey, DfEE, 1998*).

71 per cent of us think that learning can lead to a better quality of life (*Attitudes to Learning, Campaign for Learning/MORI, 1996*).

> 93 per cent of us believe that it is never too late to learn (*Attitudes to Learning, Campaign for Learning/MORI, 1996*).

During the last century we have moved from the 'industrial age' through to the 'information age' and then to the 'knowledge age'. The key to achieving success today is our ability to obtain, assimilate and apply the right knowledge effectively. Employers will no longer judge you solely on your previous qualifications; they will also assess your capacity to learn and adapt in the future.

Learning is not just about economic success, however; it is the key to achieving your full potential. Learning has the power to transform us and make us more successful in all aspects of our personal lives. It can enable us to solve problems and change our attitudes, and it can also make us more interesting to be around. Learning can be very challenging, but also great fun.

If you are responsible for training in your workplace, or if you are an employer yourself, then this book is also for you. Hopefully, this book will give you some ideas on how to improve your staff's performance and morale, and keep them motivated for the sake of the business.

What do we mean by learning, training and development?

Many of us would say that learning is a collection of facts and ideas that we gain at school and keep adding to throughout our lives, but there is more to learning than collecting information. It is the process we go through when we are obtaining new knowledge, skills, habits or values. We do this by gaining experience, reflection, study or instruction. This leads us to change the way we think and the way we act. In short, learning changes our lives by improving our understanding.

What does this tell us about learning?

»   Most of the significant learning in our lives comes from what we do. Learning is not something separate from everyday life, but is gained through action.

» Learning is not just about receiving instructions. It is also an activity in which learners participate and are actively involved.

» Learning can bring about a change in behaviour which may well be permanent; for example, it can increase our ability to perform tasks or skills, or it can change our attitude or interests.

» Learning can increase our knowledge and skills, but, in some circumstances, we can adjust our learning to deal with new situations (e.g. if we changed our job, we would have to learn extra skills).

What do you think about learning new things? Some people are very resistant to the idea and think that they will find it difficult because they performed poorly at school. Others consider themselves to be too old, or not bright enough, or they are too stressed. Usually, people who have these viewpoints see learning as coming only from school or college, books or formal training sessions. But all of us are learning all the time – it is a natural process!

So what is training? This is the process we go through to enable us to learn in a planned way. When we think of training we may automatically think of a formal process, with a trainer in a training room or classroom, often supported by materials such as handouts. But this is just one type of training. There are many different methods. Not all involve classrooms (e.g. on-the-job training) and some do not even involve a trainer at all (e.g. open learning).

What is development? Training is often seen as part of a longer-term process than just one-off events, hence the term 'training and development'. By 'development', we mean the learning of skills and knowledge over the longer term. There is often no instant fix – you would not expect to come back from a coaching course and say, 'I'm now a coach!' Such a course would provide a framework for you to understand what coaching is about. Over time, with the right support, you would develop in the coaching role.

For you, training will definitely improve your earning capacity and your quality of life. But there are also major benefits for your employer (or prospective employer), as will be revealed in the coming chapters.

Employment in the 21st century

Around 26 million people are in paid employment in the UK. The majority are based in offices, shops, hospitals, schools and colleges. If you are thinking of changing your career, here is an outline of the main sectors, to help you decide which area you would prefer to work in.

» **Manufacturing**

In 1964, almost 50 per cent of the working population had jobs directly associated with making things. This is now down to 14 per cent of employees, but there are still opportunities for a career. Large-scale modern manufacturing tends to be very hi-tech and has to lead the way in innovation to compete and survive against international competition, so it may be an exciting place to work. Modern manufacturers are the key to the UK's economic future; for example, industries such as pharmaceuticals, biotechnology, aerospace, automotive, electronics and chemicals. Moreover, with fewer people studying subjects such as engineering, maths and science, manufacturing may be looking at severe skill shortages in the near future. You may consider this as a career option if you have a leaning towards these subjects and you want to be involved in the production of material goods.

» **Service industries**

As factories have closed or become automated, most of the replacement work has involved providing services of one kind or another. Service industries have, and continue, to increase their needs for staff. In the private sector this is particularly the case in transport, distribution, hotels and catering. You may be attracted to the service sector because of the opportunities available in a vocation that interests you.

» Public sector

About 20 per cent of all jobs are in the public sector, which is the major part of the service sector. This covers a vast array of tasks crucial to the running of the country, including jobs in local and central government, teaching, medicine, social work, the armed forces and the emergency services. More than half of the jobs are in health and education. The overall numbers working in this sector are decreasing – except in health and education – due to government policy and because many functions are being contracted out to the private and voluntary sectors.

You may be attracted to the public sector because you feel that you can make a positive difference or be of practical help to people, or because you are happier working within formal structures where your role is well defined.

» Small businesses

Most firms in the UK are small businesses. 95 per cent of small businesses employ between one and 49 people. Next are small-to medium-sized businesses – also known as 'SMEs'. There are around 27,000 of these, employing 50 to 249 people.

A small business may attract you if you prefer to work in a small team with relatively informal structures, where you may need to turn your hand to a wide variety of tasks.

» Large businesses

These employ more than 250 people. There are only 7,000 of them in the UK. Some are international companies, and you may work in a division of an even larger multinational group. The jobs available will be wide ranging and many will be specialised.

You may be attracted to large businesses because of the opportunities available in a vocation that interests you or because you are happier working within formal structures where your role is well defined.

» The voluntary and community sector

This sector is a favourite choice among people who want a

career change, although more people are beginning to join the sector at the start of their careers. It comprises over 500,000 paid staff, and this figure is growing, partly due to the government awarding contracts. It employs more than the farming or car industries. A wide range of roles and ways of working are available. The largest charities have jobs which are comparable with many found in the private sector, such as accountants, marketing and public relations officers, social workers, campaigners, lawyers and scientific advisers. Voluntary organisations now have to run in a similar way to businesses, whether they are large or small, in order to survive. In recent years they have come to be referred to as 'not for profit' (NfP) organisations. They are independent from government and business, they do not distribute profits to shareholders, and they exist to benefit their members or others in their area of work.

You may be attracted to this sector because you are in sympathy with the aims and objectives of the charity or welfare group, or you want a job which helps further your personal ideals or fits in with your values. You may be able to enter initially as a volunteer – see Chapter 1 for more information.

Other trends in employment

It is worth noting other 21st century trends in employment and the implications for your training and development.

» The knowledge economy

In recent years the term 'knowledge economy' has been coined by government, businesses and economists. In essence, this term has been used to recognise that knowledge and skills are crucial to the success of the economy. It is generally agreed that a knowledge-based economic revolution is taking place. In this modern economy, wealth creation and rising prosperity depend increasingly upon the application of knowledge. Location, raw materials and the availability of capital used to be the main sources of competitive advantage, but now it is skills, knowledge and creativity which make the difference.

» **Part-time employment**

Already almost a quarter of the workforce works part time. A high proportion of these jobs are concentrated in care, catering and office work and there are far fewer in areas such as construction and manufacturing. Companies are employing growing armies of part-time, temporary or seasonal staff. Some people opt to work part time for personal or domestic reasons, such as childcare, while others may want to cut down their hours to study part time to improve their skills and qualifications, particularly if their employer does not provide them with opportunities for study.

» **Self-employment**

Approximately three million people are self-employed in the UK, and this figure is growing. Industries that have dominated the increase are real estate, letting agents and construction. Firms are also becoming increasingly reliant on self-employed consultants, many of whom once had full-time posts with the same organisations. Consultants are contracted by local authorities, small businesses or voluntary organisations so they can draw on areas of expertise that the companies may not have in house. Others have seen good business opportunities by becoming self-employed in the trade sector. Full-time self-employment can be very time-consuming and may limit your opportunities to undertake training, although some of the on-the-job training ought to be considered, and hiring a coach or a mentor would certainly be a good idea. Part-time self-employment can present the same opportunities as part-time employment.

» **Portfolio working**

Increasing numbers of people have a 'portfolio' of two, three or even four jobs which they do in the course of a week. Some may do this out of choice, and others out of financial necessity. This may apply, for example, to people working in small businesses or the voluntary sector, where the organisation does not have the resources to employ separate staff for different functions so it either employs staff part time or gives them multiple roles. Some people may include self-employment as one or more of their jobs. If you want to get experience in a 'flexible' firm such as this, you will need to work hard to get noticed. Systematic on-the-job training and apprenticeships may not be available. You will need to use your own initiative to discover what opportunities are out there, and keep more than one opening in mind at the same time.

» **Home working**

About one million people in the UK are now home or tele-workers. This has become more possible nowadays because of information technology; for example, the use of wireless-enabled laptops for internet access. Most of the work is in office or professional occupations. If you do work from home, there is a danger that the boundaries between work and home life may get muddied. You will need to be well organised and self-disciplined, but as you are likely to have more control over your day-to-day working than other employees, you may be able to allow time for learning.

Why learning more will help your career

Employers often use high-flown phrases such as 'investing in people' and 'people being our most valuable asset'. They may be seen as management clichés designed to keep staff motivated, but, nowadays, there is more to them than that. There is a powerful business case for staff training and development, and employers need to develop their employees' skills. But why is this?

» **The rapid change in technology and the jobs people do**

With accelerating changes in technology and work systems, many traditional industrial and office jobs have disappeared altogether. Others have changed radically and still continue to change. New jobs have been created, particularly in the service or information-based industries. Against this backcloth employers cannot always be sure that there will be enough external candidates with the appropriate skills to fill their vacancies. There are two solutions to this problem. One is to recruit people with potential and train them, and the other is to provide enough opportunities to enable existing staff to keep their skills up to date.

» Skill shortages

Due to the above, there is a very high demand for skill and knowledge-based jobs and a greater demand for skilled workers, and a reduced requirement for unskilled labour. This is the cause of the skill shortages so evident in countries like the UK, even at times when unemployment has been high. The problem is made worse as a result of the greater complexity of jobs and the decreasing numbers of young people entering the workforce (far fewer children were born in the 1960s and 1970s than in the immediate post-war period). Employers also take the view that at present many school leavers do not have useful qualifications. This skills gap can best be overcome by an expansion of training, retraining and staff development opportunities.

» Changes in the composition and expectations of the workforce

Being aware of these changes, many employees – especially those recruited over the past 15 years or so – are keen to keep their skills up to date. They see that they need 'portable' skills to keep them employable if and when their current job changes or vanishes. In the past people expected their education and training to last them a lifetime, but those days have gone. Employers who respond to this need are more likely to retain their staff, and indeed encourage high-calibre new staff to join.

» Pressures for improvement in the quality of products and services

Many employers, because of pressure from competition or government legislation, have developed their own quality assurance systems in recent years, either by creating them from scratch or by adapting one of the established off-the-shelf systems, such as Investors in People (see page xix for more information). They have also improved their procedures in areas such as health and safety and data protection. This has made staff more individually accountable, and has heightened the need for training, even for those who may be regarded as less skilled, such as receptionists, care assistants and sales assistants.

» Keeping the competitive edge

Research has shown that training and development is vital to employers in encouraging staff to stay, and to continue to work to a high standard, manage technological change, and fend off the effects of skill shortages. This helps them keep the competitive edge. Log on to the website of the Chartered Institute of Personnel and Development (CIPD), the professional body for those involved in the management and development of people (see *Useful contacts* for details). The need to keep UK industry competitive is the reasoning behind the government's strategy on workplace learning. Investment in training helps ensure a flexible workforce, which is able to make rapid adjustment to change.

» Government policies

Government policy has had a major impact on training and development, particularly by encouraging new partnerships between employers and educational organisations, as well as trade unions and voluntary and community organisations. Schemes and initiatives such as the University for Industry, the Learning and Skills Councils, National Vocational Qualifications (NVQs) and lifelong learning all exist to encourage employers to take training and development seriously, sometimes with financial incentives.

On 22 March 2005, the government published its second Skills White Paper, *Skills: Getting on in business, getting on at work*. This sets out a revised skills strategy (see www.dfes.gov.uk/skillsstrategy) and it includes the development of the National Employer Training Programme (NETP). This provides a package of free training in the workplace, designed for employers and delivered to suit their operational needs. Also, the government has appointed Sir Digby Jones to the role of

Skills Envoy to head up the drive to ensure that the UK does not get left behind by a lack of skills within its adult population. The former director of the Confederation of British Industry insists that he will remain fully independent of the government in fighting to ensure that employers develop the skills of their workforce, but he is insistent that if skill levels are not improved in the next three years, whatever government is in power, it will introduce regulations to force change. The Skills Envoy takes the view that a lack of training will 'kill the enterprise culture in the UK'.

Test the employer

There are certain key questions you should be asking if you want to establish how seriously an employer takes training and development. These questions can be asked of not only your current employer (if you have one), but also any prospective employer.

» **Has it reached the Investors in People Standard?**

The Investors in People Standard (IIP) demonstrates that the employer has good practices in employee training and development, and is working to develop its ways of working through its people. If the employer has been awarded this standard, it is a good indication that it takes training and development seriously. However, it is still vital to ask all the other questions below.

Employers can apply to be assessed for an IIP. The IIP assessors visit personally and assess over a period of time (depending on the size of the organisation). Part of their assessment involves interviewing a cross-section of employees at all levels in the organisation. If the employer reaches the standard, it is allowed to publicise this fact and it can use the IIP logo. Every three years the employer is assessed by means of a repeat visit to ensure that the standard is still being applied.

For more information, log on to the IIP website (see *Useful contacts* for details).

» **Does it invest in training and development?**

If the answer to this is no, then either the employer has a lot of work to do – and needs to buy this book as a start – or it is not recognising what it does as training and development. This is not as strange as it may sound. Training is often seen as providing courses, for example, rather than helping staff to learn on the job. Any activity that helps staff to learn can be classed as training and development.

» **Who decides what training is to happen, when and for whom?**

The answer to this is another indicator of the importance given to training. It is more likely to be taken seriously if the person making the decisions has high status in the company, is empowered to influence line managers to ensure that his staff are properly trained, and has been able to secure and maintain a reasonably sized training budget. The answer also helps to reveal whether the company has a well-worked-out strategy and policy, whether there is an implemented training plan, and whether training is made available to all staff or only to some.

» **Does any learning take place informally or on the job? If it does, is it recognised as such?**

This question teases out whether recognition is given to development that takes place outside of the training room. Learning by imitation 'on the job', providing that it is well structured and monitored, can be a very powerful learning strategy in the workplace. See Chapter 2, *On-the-job training* on page 38. A lot of NVQs, Open College Network and other accredited learning also takes place on the job – see Chapter 2, including *National Vocational Qualifications (NVQs)* on page 40 and *Open learning* on page 43.

» **Does it have any arrangements for flexible learning?**

Not all training consists of formal courses. You can learn numerous skills by teaching yourself through self-help training packs, online learning and on-the-job learning. However, you will be likely to make better progress if your employer is prepared to encourage and support you to learn flexibly. This can happen in many different ways; for example, by the employer providing coaches or mentors, or time off for private study, or access to in-work libraries or study centres, or a range of different courses that you can select from to suit your needs. Some employers will have links with Learn Direct, the business arm of the government agency (see Chapter 6), or they will participate in the 'Learning through Work' scheme to help you achieve a university qualification while you work (see Chapter 5).

» **How is training and development planned? Does it 'just happen' or is it systematic?**

Employers should have a planned programme for future training. Many employers, if they invest in training at all, tend to do so on a spasmodic, reactive basis, or in response to a crisis. This is not good news. A properly worked out strategy, linked to the company's business plan, is best.

» **Are there any policies that refer specifically to training and development? Are these implemented?**

The existence of a written down policy or one overall policy is good news in that it should give you some confidence that what is said is actually implemented. Also, if in practice training and development is taking a back seat, then drawing attention to the policy may help you get the training you need. It is not uncommon for employers to have splendid policies and training manuals that get ignored to gather dust on the HR Manager's shelf.

» **Is any recognition given to Continuing Professional Development (CPD)?**

CPD means, in essence, facilitating a rolling programme of training and development, a continual process of personal growth, to improve the capability and realise the full potential of professional people at work. This can be achieved by obtaining and developing a wide range of knowledge, skills and experience, which are not normally acquired during initial training or routine work. The employer should support and encourage CPD for professionals, and ideally for other staff as well.

» **Is training only offered in house, or are external providers used?**

The use of external providers can enhance training provision even for large companies, since there are usually limitations on what can be done in house. The wider the variety of provision, the more likely it is that training can be tailor-made to your needs.

» **How do the staff feel about the training? Is it seen as a reward or a punishment, a right or a necessary evil?**

We have all worked with people who have the attitude that they know the job inside out and there is nothing new to learn. To them a training event is a 'jolly', something to get out of the workday routine. Where this attitude is prevalent in the company, then it is likely that the problem stems from senior management attitudes and a lack of a learning culture. In order for it to become a learning organisation, your company needs to develop its culture, policies and practices to encourage continual improvement and learning at all levels.

» **What kinds of external factors affect the training and development organised?**

This reveals how flexible and responsive the training programme is, whether the company takes on board external changes, such as new legislation or government policies; changes affecting customers, suppliers or other stakeholders; technological development; or changes to the local or national economy. A rigid training programme that does not take account of these issues, or ignores them until a set review date, will score low on this question.

» **Is there an adequate budget?**

If the employer scores well on the above, this may mean nothing if it does not have enough money allocated to the training budget. How much is enough will depend on the nature of the business, but if it is insufficient to meet the workplace's training needs, then it is not enough. The problem is that many companies invest well in training and development when business is booming but this budget can be the first to be cut in lean times. However, given that training and development is the lifeblood of any company, this approach can be seen to be short-sighted.

» Will it let me have time off work to receive training?

As part of a training policy, the employer may let you take time off work to receive training; for example, to allow you to go on a course. Some may also allow study leave to allow you to complete assignments or reading at home or at a study centre. Clearly this is good practice as it can ease the pressures on your time.

> **NOTE**
>
> If you are aged 16 or 17, are not in full-time education, and are not qualified to level 2 of the National Qualifications Framework (NQF) (see Chapter 3), you have the legal right to paid time off work to study or train. This will help you gain skills and achieve a nationally recognised qualification. If you are aged 18, you also have the right to complete study or training which you have already started.
>
> The study and training can be undertaken in the workplace, on the job or elsewhere on site; in a college with an approved training provider; through open or distance learning; or elsewhere.
>
> The amount of time that you can have off will depend on your circumstances, taking into account the requirements of the course or training as well as your employer's business needs. You will be entitled to payment for the time off at the appropriate hourly rate. If your employer unreasonably refuses to give you time off for study or training, or fails to pay you, you can take your complaint to an employment tribunal. More information can be found from Connexions at www.dfes.gov.uk/tfst.

» **Will it pay for any of my training?**

It is important to know the circumstances, if any, in which you will be reimbursed for your training expenses, including the cost of travelling and maybe overnight accommodation to enable you to attend. If your training needs have been identified with the employer, you would normally expect its policy to allow reimbursement.

» **How does it assess and prioritise my training needs?**

This question helps establish which of the methods of identifying and assessing training needs the employer uses, if any. In order to ensure that your needs are properly understood, evaluated and applied, it is good practice for the employer to use more than just one method. You will also need to know how your needs are prioritised; for example, some employers may invest more training on new recruits and less on older hands. A preferred approach would allow you the training to help you develop your skills, regardless of your length of service.

» **What support is available to help me learn?**

It is not sufficient for the employer to simply organise training for you and leave you to get on with it, even if it is highly relevant and it meets your needs well. Good practice requires the employer to put into place support to help you get the best out of the training, beyond administrative support. You should also benefit from having access to a coach to help you identify your learning needs, and to assist you in finding the most suitable training options; then to provide informed support and guidance to help you develop skills, grow in confidence and competence, and keep you at the peak of your abilities. Your line manager should carry out some of these functions as well as proactively support you by recognising when you have to be absent from duties to attend training. Support is particularly vital if you are undertaking on-the-job training, distance learning or computer-based learning. Having a mentor will also help you talk through decisions affecting your future.

» **Is the structure of the workplace geared to training and development?**

The structure is the way things are organised, such as the levels of responsibilities, task allocation, decision making, etc. This information is usually written down – appearing in such places as staff written particulars of employment, the staff handbook, policy and procedure manuals, training plans and company policies. What is said about training and development will indicate the employer's attitude to it.

» **What does the culture of the company tell you about training and development?**

The culture is the set of norms, values, ideas and beliefs held about the way things are done (or not done!) in the organisation. Although some aspects of culture are expressed in written form, a great deal is implicit. Culture affects the management style, which is how the managers manage others, their attitudes, points of view, ways of thinking and working, and how they form relationships. This, in turn, can affect the approach to training and development.

WORKPLACE CULTURES

Here are the four workplace cultures. Of course, these are generalisations. Overall, you may find that one of the four best describes your organisation, although there may be a separate culture (a sub-culture) in a department or a branch. Although these types of culture may not exist in 'pure' form, they may prove useful in working out what you can expect from different employers.

1. Power culture

Characteristics: Autocratic or paternalistic. People are told what they have to achieve and their actions are judged on results. At best this means people know where they stand, but they usually follow orders because they fear the consequences of not doing so.

Types of companies: Start-up situations, hotels, restaurants, media organisations, political groups, emergency services, airline services, investment banks and property companies. Within an organisation, power sub-cultures may include the top management positions, the finance department, production, and the sales and marketing departments.

Nature of training preferred: Risk taking, trial and error, self-development, apprenticeship, and the discovery method of instruction.

2. Role culture

Characteristics: Stability and control. Heavy reliance on the use of systems and procedures so that all staff have clear roles, thus reducing conflict and confusion.

Types of companies: Retail industries, banking, the civil service and local government, schools, hospitals and the motor industry. Within an organisation, role sub-cultures may include the wages section, the secretarial system, office services, production and quality control.

Nature of training preferred: Highly organised training where risk is kept to a minimum; objective, structured and standardised training for the role rather than the individual; counselling to correct deficiencies; skills training to provide a standard service; case studies; business games; education to achieve qualifications and status within the organisation.

3. Achievement culture

Characteristics: This culture features self-development and achievement on the part of individual staff. People tend to be driven by a sense of value or a vision. Adaptability is valued and a problem solving team culture is promoted to maintain the flexibility required.

Types of companies: Organisations within this culture deal with innovation. They are the home of the expert working within a team, such as research teams, management consultancies, aerospace companies, construction companies and software houses. Within an organisation they could be the research and development team, corporate planning, computer programmers, recruitment, project teams and task forces.

Nature of training preferred: Informality and practical relevance is preferred; for example, coaching, discovery training where there is a clear practical application, training in skills to achieve the task in hand, goal-centred training and group/teamwork.

4. Club culture

Characteristics: This culture is based on a sense of community. It is co-operative, caring and responsive. The main aim is to seek mutuality, integration and a high-quality service. People are empowered by mutual trust, co-operation, understanding and assistance.

Types of companies: This type of culture is usually found in small voluntary organisations, partnerships, barristers' chambers, small family firms, small consultancies, or spiritually or religious-orientated communities. Sub-cultures within organisations can exist among professionals and trainers and are mostly people employed because of their special experience and skills.

Nature of training preferred: Mentoring and coaching, creative learning, experimentation, self-development, learner-centred training, intuitive learning, and learning skills which can be transferred.

It is important that the training methods match the culture in any company. If there is a mismatch between culture and management style, and training methods, things can go horribly wrong. Management may ignore or not support the training effort, or it may highlight any shortcomings in the training. This, in turn, will reflect badly on the trainer and the learner, or staff may see the training as irrelevant to their daily work. All this defeats the whole object of training and development.

» **What are the attitudes of the senior people?**

Although culture and structure sets the tone, individuals in key positions can have a big influence on the kinds of training and development that take place and what status it is given, through their unique values, attitudes, and patterns of behaviour. How do the senior people in your company stand on training and development?

» Can I have accredited training?

Sometimes, you may take training with a company and then apply for a new job, only to find that the new company does not recognise your achievements. If you are able to carry out training which is accredited, you may avoid this problem, because it will be externally recognised – provided, of course, that you completed it successfully. So the employer who offers accredited training scores well here. Depending on your occupation there may be set standards in place (National Occupational Standards (NOS)) with agreed competences. These standards allow trainers to identify the current competence of individuals or a group of staff against a set of clearly defined standards for their particular occupational area. If you are in one of these occupations, there is all the more reason for your employer to offer accredited training. A further benefit of standards is that they provide opportunities for learners to obtain NVQs as they are designed to complement the NVQ framework (or Scottish Vocational Qualifications (SVQs) in Scotland) – see *Occupational standards* in Chapter 3.

» How will I be rewarded if I undergo training?

You hope that your employer will view your training favourably and that this will lead to an increase in pay, an offer for a better job, or perhaps a promotion. However, if the employer does not consider these as options, all is not lost as the skills you have developed will surely impress any prospective new employer, especially if your training was accredited.

» Is the work environment conducive to learning?

Many employers fall at this hurdle, even those who have really good training policies in place. You are probably familiar with the litany of issues that beset workplaces around the country, for example:

» Everyone being preoccupied with their tasks in hand, half watching their emails coming in and constantly answering the phone. The routines dominate to such an extent that nobody has time to reflect on what they are doing, to develop in their job, to consider whether there are more effective ways of working, or to help support their colleagues. Employers who take learning seriously promote a learning culture to try to counter this tendency.

» Tribalism in the workplace, where a big 'them and us' relationship exists between teams, and where office politics dominates. Often this tribalism has its roots in past practices or influences of dominant personalities (not just those in management positions). As a result, communication between teams is poor, colleagues in 'rival' teams will not support each other, and most staff in a team are preoccupied with what the 'others' may be up to. Again, this is all to the detriment of workplace learning and the adoption of a creative approach.

» Management that does not support learning in the workplace. Some managers are entirely focused on achievement of tasks, allowing their staff little or no scope for reflection, on-the-job learning or coming up with ideas on how the job may be carried out more effectively. Usually, these managers are not operating in isolation, but they are supported by a culture that does not encourage learning.

» High levels of stress. In Britain, statistics suggest that the total cost of stress to industry is between three and 3.5 per cent of gross national product, with more than 40 million days lost each year to stress-related illnesses. Any form of training and development is likely to be rendered less effective if the learner is suffering from negative stress. Employers have to tackle its root causes if they are to improve staff receptiveness to learning.

» Fear stalks many workplaces. This is linked to negative stress and arises from fears such as loss of job, status, promotion or bonuses. Where staff members live in fear they become more defensive, aggressive, and much less creative and open to learning. There is a culture of backbiting, resistance to change, corridor gossip, lack of honesty and hidden agendas. Again, the root causes need to be tackled if things are to improve.

Chapter 1

Practical steps for you to help yourself

Explore possible careers

Maybe you are looking for your first job, or you just want a new challenge. Perhaps you have been made redundant, or you have not changed jobs in a while and you feel like the workplace has changed. If any of these circumstances apply to you, then a careers adviser can help. He can advise you on how you can update your skills and help you think of the work options open to you. There are different careers advice services depending on your needs and situation.

If you are aged under 19 (England and Wales only), you can use the Connexions Service and speak to a personal adviser at your local Connexions centre. To find your local centre, log on to www.connexions-direct.com or look for one in your local phone book. Alternatively, you can contact a Connexions direct adviser by phone – see *Useful contacts*.

If you are over 19, there may be a free careers guidance service in your area and your local Connexions Service, or your local Jobcentre Plus office, may be able to advise you. If you are a university student or have recently graduated, your university, or the one in the area where you live, should be able to help. There are many commercial careers guidance services which you can find in your local *Yellow Pages* or phone book, or on the internet. Otherwise, look for local

eers guidance providers. There may be a charge for
in some cases, so check before committing yourself.

In addition, Learn Direct (see *Useful contacts* for details) can help you choose a course or work out your next step. Its lifelong learning advisers can help you or put you in touch with a local careers adviser (you can call Learn Direct on 0800 100 900). Calls are in confidence and impartial, with advice on your options including how you can change your career, update your skills, get a promotion, do some self-development and get a qualification.

Information on the many careers related to occupations can be found on the internet or from reference books. For a summary of sources and career possibilities, see Chapter 9.

There is also a UK qualifications database at the website of the UK National Reference Point for Vocational Qualifications at www. uknrp.org.uk. One way to find a vocational course in the UK is to use one of the following sites:

» Hot Courses – www.hotcourses.com.

» Hobsons ('Springboard') – www.springboard.co.uk.

» Floodlight (courses in London) – www.floodlight.co.uk.

Find out how to update your skills and qualifications

If you want more opportunities with the company you work for, or you are looking for a better job elsewhere, you may need to update your skills.

Find out which skills are needed in the type of work you have in mind. Look at job adverts, trade journals or contact any relevant Sector Skills Council (SSC) (you can find a list of the appropriate SSCs in Chapter 9 and the addresses in *Useful contacts*) and professional or industry body. A search online may reveal more sources. You can also search for a course via Learn Direct and other sources referred to in this book, depending on the qualification you are looking for (see Chapter 3).

You could consider looking beyond your work experience and develop the skills you have gained from your domestic life, hobbies or voluntary work, which can also be useful for career development. For example, teamwork and leadership skills can be developed through coaching a local football or netball team. Organisational and planning skills can grow from caring for or bringing up children. You could improve your written skills with a creative writing course or get experience in book-keeping by helping a local charity. For more information on volunteering, see *Do voluntary work* on page 7.

If you are not sure of the skills you would like to develop, you could spend time trying out different options. If you have time, you could, for example, create a two-year learning plan for your own development and interests. This could include a combination of work-related and fun activities; for example, you could aim to gain a Certificate in Marketing (approved by the Chartered Institute of Marketing), learn how to manage Excel spreadsheets to intermediate level, get an introduction to snowboarding or attend Italian cookery classes.

If you feel that you need help with your reading, writing and maths, there are courses available all over the country. Many of these are free of charge. (See Chapter 4, *Skills for Life* on page 69.)

For other help and advice, try the Department for Children, Schools and Families' website, the Aimhigher website, the government's website www.direct.gov.uk, and the Hot Courses website (see *Useful contacts* for details).

Network

A great way to improve your job and training opportunities is to network. What is networking? If you think of the ways in which you first form friendships with people, it is all about finding something in common, entering into a conversation or discussion, and offering and receiving help and support. It is a process of building relationships. Networking involves the same process, but in the professional world it is about actively fostering contacts with the aim to:

» make people more aware of your existence and what you can offer – either now or potentially;

» obtain information from others about training or job opportunities that will be of benefit to you.

Here are some ingredients that will make networking work for you.

» **Always be on the lookout for opportunities to network.**

These can arise spontaneously, so try not to miss any chances. They may be casual meetings by the coffee machine, gatherings that take place before or after a formal meeting, training sessions, informal chats with colleagues, even starting up conversations on the train or at the station. These may be opportunities to make initial contact which you can follow up later.

» **Nothing ventured, nothing gained.**

Do not hesitate to contact others for fear of imposing or asking for help. The reality is that most people are happy to do something for someone else, if asked. So be bold. Strike up conversations where you can. You will soon get the message if the person does not want to talk to you.

» **Make regular and consistent follow-ups.**

If the contact welcomes your first approach and things go well, he will want to hear about your progress. Thank him and make plans to meet him again, or at least take his email address or phone number and arrange to get in touch. Keep him aware of your progress and ask him about his plans. This process of nurturing contacts will sustain and enhance your career.

» **Exchange information.**

If you can offer the contact something in exchange, this will encourage him. For example, you may be able to offer names of other contacts to help him, or provide him with a recommendation or other information.

» **Back up your offer with action.**

If possible, do more than just give him information. Offer to take action to help the contact if you can; for example, by offering to find out more, or by getting him an introduction if it is possible.

» **Have a plan.**

Before networking, consider what you need from a contact and if there is any information you can offer him. Planning is vital if you want to make the best of networking. Whether you are approaching a colleague, a friend, a family member or stranger, how you present your purpose will make the difference between a satisfying or unsatisfying experience.

» **Do your homework.**

For every meeting try to find out as much as you can about the person you will be meeting; for example, his background, including his occupation, style, affiliations and interests.

If you are looking for an opportunity within a company or other organisation, you will need to research it as well, and possibly the industry of which it is part. Become familiar with the organisation's products, structure, services, financial status, competitors, reputation and any recent major changes that have occurred. You can do this through the following methods:

» The public library (books, periodicals, magazines, trade journals, etc.).

» Literature from the company's public relations department. Call and explain that you have a scheduled meeting and would like background information.

» Information on the company's attitude and policies on training and development (see the Introduction, *Test the employer* on page xix).

5

» Annual reports. Contact the company and it will send you one. You should also find a pdf version on the company's website.

» The internet and other sources of electronic information. Be sure to check out the company's website.

In order to network effectively, you need to do the following:

» Learn about unpublished job or training opportunities.

» Be referred to an opportunity you did not know about.

» Keep current with trends and personalities in your field.

» Gain greater perspective about your job area or interest.

» Increase your field of contacts so that you can broaden your search (the more people who know who you are, know what you do, and what you want to do, the more likely you are to connect with interested decision makers).

» Learn about the problems and needs in organisations, so that you can work out what you can offer. Through networking you may be able to propose a position, or meet a manager who will see you as the walking solution to his problems.

How to network for a new role

Call, email or write to the person, refer to the situation/place/person that brought you together. Set goals for the meeting. Relieve any tension by stressing that you did not request the meeting to ask for a job. Explain that you are making a change and you are here to explore ideas about your industry and your next career step.

» **Set the agenda.**

Concisely, lay out what you want to discuss. (You can only do this if you have a clear idea of what you need to say and ask beforehand.) Be brief and stick to the point. Ensure that the person clearly understands his role and explain how he can help you.

» **Summarise and discuss your skills and relevant experience.**

Describe some of your recent accomplishments and highlight those skills, strengths and experiences to those who you believe the contact would be most responsive to. Use examples. Make known your career goals and objectives.

» **Encourage dialogue.**

Ask questions, and draw information from the contact. Get feedback on your job search plan, objectives and updated CV.

If the contact mentions obstacles you might face in reaching your career goal, ask for advice on how to overcome them. If he cannot help you, ask for the name of someone who can, by saying, 'Who do you think may be able to give me the information I need?'.

» **Ask questions.**

Prepare key questions in advance and the more specific they are, the better. After asking them, listen to the answers to ensure two-way communication. Acknowledge and respond to what the person is saying. By following his cues, you can determine what he may consider impressive. Observe carefully. If the contact shows signs of boredom or uneasiness, change the subject.

Do voluntary work

Local charities and other voluntary organisations may welcome you to work for them as a volunteer. If you join them, you may find that you have more opportunities to gain experience and new skills than you would in a paid job, so this is a great way of improving your CV. Employers often recognise that you can learn new skills which are useful for career progression, such as teamworking, decision making and communication, and many jobs that you are looking for can be found in volunteering, such as marketing, fund-raising, media, information technology (IT), etc.

It is also a great way to use your knowledge and skills to help others, and at the same time give you a new experience and opportunity to improve your confidence. In many cases, nowadays, this may lead to a qualification; for example, you may be able to arrange to have your experience accredited.

There are a wide variety of volunteering opportunities so it is worth thinking about what you want to do and what you want to get out of it. These may include advice work, helping children, organising a fringe theatre group or lending a hand on a community newspaper. If you feel that you cannot give your time on a regular basis, there are voluntary projects and holidays that may interest you, which may include opportunities abroad and in the UK.

Volunteering can be an attractive option as you can:

» help others and your local community;

» feel good about yourself;

» meet new people;

» take part in something which is important to you;

» make a difference;

» do something you enjoy;

» develop your interests;

» learn new skills;

» get a chance to practise skills you have recently learned;

» gain experience and improve your CV;

» boost your job prospects.

Although you will not receive payment as a volunteer, the voluntary organisations will usually pay you expenses to cover your travel, and possibly the cost of someone caring for your child or dependent relative. Your training costs should also be covered.

Businesses and the public sector are becoming increasingly interested in how their own employees can become involved in volunteering. Many and varied programmes are being set up to assist employees to volunteer, whether during work hours or in their own time. This is called 'employer supported volunteering'. According to the Home Office Citizenship Survey: People, Families and Communities in England, 18 per cent of employees work for employers who have schemes for volunteers and of these 37 per cent volunteer as part of these schemes.

You could encourage your employer to take part, and then you may be able to volunteer with its backing.

Despite a lot of voluntary work taking place during office hours, there are still some opportunities for you to volunteer in the evenings or weekends if you work full time. Alternatively, if you have no employment or family commitments, you may want to consider a period of full-time volunteering either in the UK or abroad.

Training opportunities for volunteers

If you want to volunteer to help boost your career, think carefully about the skills and experience you need. When voluntary organisations are recruiting, they may ask you what your particular interests and skills are, so they can see how they can accommodate you. Even if you are applying for a specific vacancy, do not be afraid to be upfront about your own requirements. Although the organisation will want to recruit you to further its own objectives and deliver its services, it should not lose sight of the fact that you will need to benefit as well.

Volunteering can give you a broad range of learning opportunities:

»   Many volunteer placements will allow you to study and develop your 'Key Skills' – the skills you need to get on in the workplace, in learning and in life.

»   Some volunteers receive vocational training in specialist areas, such as social care, working with the elderly, or working with children.

»   Some roles require specific training, such as volunteering as a special constable with a local police force.

» Some voluntary organisations recruit many volunteers in a wide variety of roles, so it will often be possible for you to sample several roles and work out what you like best.

» If you show commitment, the voluntary organisation may be more likely to give you responsibilities much earlier on than you if you were in a paid post.

Where to apply

Some volunteering roles will suit you more than others so it is worth thinking about why you want to volunteer, how much time you have available and what skills you can offer.

You can search for opportunities in your area. Usually, there will be one centre you can contact to register as a volunteer and look for vacancies. The name of this centre will differ from area to area; it may be called the Council for Voluntary Service (CVS), Voluntary Action, the Volunteer Centre or the Volunteer Development Agency. These centres also promote and develop volunteering and voluntary organisations in their areas.

If you have a clear idea of where you would like to work, you could contact an organisation direct, such as the local Citizens Advice Bureau or the Samaritans.

You can find your local centre and also a lot more about volunteering opportunities (in the UK and abroad) from the National Association for Voluntary and Community Action (NAVCA), Volunteering England, Volunteer Development Scotland, Volunteering Wales, the Volunteer Development Agency (for Northern Ireland), V Inspired (for young people in England aged 16 to 25) and the universal website www.do-it.org.uk. See *Useful contacts* for details.

Log on to the Community Service Volunteers' website (www.csv.org. uk/fulltimevolunteering) and have a look at the full-time volunteering opportunities for people who want to take a gap year, improve their skills, gain work experience or just have a great time.

If you are interested in volunteering for a particular voluntary organisation, you should find that its website will contain information on opportunities and how to apply (e.g. Oxfam, Save the Children, the RSPCA).

If you are worried about losing welfare benefits while volunteering, take advice from the Jobcentre Plus office from where you claim, or contact the local Citizens Advice Bureau (in the phone book) or use the Citizens Advice web-based information service (www.advice guide.org.uk). Generally, if you are on Jobseeker's Allowance, you can do voluntary work so long as you continue to actively seek work and you are prepared to give up volunteering if a suitable paid job becomes available.

You should think about creating a portfolio of your achievements to prove what you have learned during your time at the organisation and then you can use it to sell yourself on your CV and at any interviews you have.

The organisations

» **Schemes for volunteering abroad**

The Project Trust is for young people aged 17 to 19 and is a gap year organisation which can help school leavers go abroad for a year's voluntary work.

Raleigh International is a youth development charity that inspires people from all backgrounds and nationalities to work together on environmental and community projects around the world. If you are aged 17 to 25, visit its website.

If volunteering abroad appeals to you, visit the Voluntary Service Overseas (VSO) website.

If you are a young person, check out the Youth for Development zone on the VSO's website. There is a range of challenging, highly rewarding projects especially for committed 18–25 year-olds based in areas such as Bangladesh, Vietnam and Uganda. Projects generally focus on improving education and quality of life within communities in deprived areas.

You will need to go through an application process including an assessment day. Successful candidates then need to fund-raise a set contribution for the trip. Do not worry, though, they have lots of ideas on how to raise the cash.

For all the details of these organisations, see *Useful contacts*.

» The Millennium Volunteers scheme

Millennium Volunteers is an initiative for young people aged 16 to 25. As a Millennium Volunteer, you volunteer your time to help others, doing what you enjoy. You could be involved in projects such as sports coaching, environmental issues, youth leadership, music and dance. To take part, just ask at the organisation you volunteer for, or for further information contact the following national bodies.

In England V runs the Millennium Volunteers scheme. V is an independent charity championing youth volunteering in England. Its aim is to inspire a new generation of young volunteers (aged 16 to 25) and enable a lasting change in the quality, quantity and diversity of youth volunteering. In Scotland, Wales and Northern Ireland the scheme is run by Volunteer Development Scotland, Volunteering Wales and the Volunteer Development Agency respectively. See *Useful contacts* for the organisations' website addresses.

After 100 hours of volunteering, you are presented with an award signed by the government minister responsible for the scheme. When you reach the target of 200 hours, you receive an Award of Excellence signed by the Secretary of State.

» Do-it!

The Do-it! website (www.do-it.org.uk) is run by YouthNet UK. You may find it useful, whatever your age, but it is primarily geared to young people under 25. The site makes it easy to search for opportunities in your area involving things that interest you at times when you are available, so finding the right project for you is easy. You will be surprised how many different kinds of volunteering there are near you.

» **Youth Action**

Youth Action is a successful and innovative approach to youth volunteering. It enables thousands of young people across the country to become active in their own time to meet other young people, gain skills, have fun and put into reality their ideas and priorities that are of benefit to their own communities. Youth Action gives young people real opportunities to play a key role in the design, delivery and evaluation of projects. See *Useful contacts* for details.

» **Volunteering Holidays**

There is an exciting range of holiday possibilities available in the UK and abroad, including conservation and charity projects. Prices vary as these usually involve paying a 'contribution' to the overall cost, and it can be expensive. However, organisations often include a fund-raising pack which can help to ease the costs or you could raise the payment in full.

» **National Trust**

If you love nature, wildlife or history, you may be interested in a conservation project holiday in beautiful settings across Britain. There are 16 Plus holidays for young people aged 16 to 18 and working holidays for people over 18.

You will be involved in hands-on conservation projects, but you will need to pay for your accommodation and food. For example, 16 Plus holidays cost £75 per week plus transport.

Here are a few examples of what you can do:

» Work in the grounds of a fallow deer sanctuary.

» Learn to rebuild dry-stone walls in an ancient abbey.

» Do hands-on work in an archaeological dig.

» Conserve woodland in the grounds of a stately home.

See *Useful contacts* for details.

» **Jubilee Sailing Trust**

This organisation offers worldwide working sailing holidays for both physically disabled and able-bodied people. No sailing experience is needed as you will be shown the ropes by your mentor and everyone looks out for everyone else. See *Useful contacts* for details.

» **Youth Leadership Scheme**

If you are between 16 to 25, you can apply to join the Youth Leadership Scheme. If your application is accepted, the cost is reduced by up to £300 and you actively fund-raise the remaining cost of the trip.

If you manage to raise more than the cost of your voyage, you will be able to use this towards a future voyage, or to sponsor another young person to take part.

Here is what you can expect during your working holiday:

» You will be paired with a suitable 'buddy', so that you can look out for each other's needs and face challenges together.

» You will spend a week or two on a tall ship, working as an active member of the crew, day and night.

» On completion of the course, you will be given a certificate as a record of your achievement.

» The course can also count as your Duke of Edinburgh Gold Residential – see page 15 for more information.

Whatever your preference, there are fun and interesting volunteering opportunities for you.

For more information, you can speak to a personal adviser at your local Connexions Centre. To find your local centre, click on the 'Local Services' icon in the footer of the website's homepage or check out your local phone book. You can also contact a Connexions Direct Adviser by using the organisation's helpline (see *Useful contacts* for details).

» **Duke of Edinburgh's Award**

The Duke of Edinburgh's Award is a good way to improve on your existing skills and learn new ones. It may also help you in your chosen career as lots of employers now regard the award as an extra qualification. You can try for an award if you are aged between 14 and 25, but all awards must be finished by the time you reach your 25th birthday.

The Duke of Edinburgh's Award is a voluntary programme of activities which you can do in your spare time. There are three different levels (gold, silver and bronze), but you do not have to do them all.

You can start the Bronze Award from the age of 14 and it will take you at least six months to complete. The Silver Award you can start from the age of 15 and it will take you at least 12 months to complete. You can start the Gold Award if you are aged 16 or over. This is the most difficult of the three awards and it will take you a minimum of 18 months to complete.

At each level there are four sections. These are:

1. Service – to encourage service to individuals and the community.

2. Skills – to encourage the discovery and development of personal interests and social and practical skills.

3. Physical recreation – to encourage participation and improvement in physical activity.

4. Expeditions – to encourage a spirit of adventure and discovery.

You have to show that you have carried out one activity for each area.

There is also an extra requirement for the Gold Award:

5. Residential project – to broaden your experience through involvement with others in a residential setting.

More details of these awards can be found on the Duke of Edinburgh's Award website (see *Useful contacts* for details).

If you are at school or college, it may run the award. You can also do the award through numerous uniformed organisations, such as the scouts, the guides, the Air Training Corps, the Army Cadet Force, the girl's brigade or even your local youth club.

If you do not know where to do the award, you can contact one of the UK Award offices by looking on the website.

» **TimeBank**

This BBC supported campaign gives you the opportunity to share your time and skills with your community. The site (see *Useful contacts* for details) allows you to register your details so you can receive a list of organisations in your area that need help, and which match your interests.

» **Student Volunteering England**

The national centre for student volunteering. See *Useful contacts* for details.

» **The Experience Corps**

An organisation working to encourage and enable people aged 50 and over to volunteer and get involved in their communities. See *Useful contacts* for details.

» **Retired and Senior Volunteer Programme (RSVP)**

This organisation promotes volunteering by older people and matches individuals with local voluntary opportunities. It operates across Great Britain with more than 5,000 volunteers and it aims to involve as many people as possible over the age of 50. See *Useful contacts* for details.

» **Reach**

It recruits people of all ages and backgrounds throughout the UK with specific business, professional, managerial or technical career experience. See *Useful contacts* for details.

» **eVolunteer.co.uk**

An online resource for recruiting volunteers. See *Useful contacts* for details.

If you are worried about losing welfare benefits while volunteering, take advice from the Jobcentre Plus office from where you claim, or contact the local Citizens Advice Bureau (in the phone book) or use the Citizens Advice web-based information service at www.advice guide.org.uk. Generally, if you are on Jobseeker's Allowance, you can do voluntary work so long as you continue to actively seek work and you are prepared to give up volunteering if a suitable paid job becomes available.

You should think about creating a portfolio of your achievements to prove what you have learned during your time at the organisation and then you can use it to sell yourself on your CV and at any interviews you have.

Use a mentor

The word 'mentor' originally comes from Greek mythology. When Odysseus, King of Ithaca went to fight the Trojan War he entrusted his son Telemachus to the care and direction of his old and trusted friend, Mentor. It was more than ten years before father and son were reunited. During the course of history the word 'mentor' has become synonymous with a trusted adviser, friend, teacher and wise person. The Oxford Dictionary definition of mentor is 'experienced and trusted adviser'.

Those who have become mentors often describe it as one of the most rewarding experiences they have ever had. Mentoring provides a wonderful learning opportunity. The mentor can take part in the development of your skills to help you build relationships within and outside the workplace. Sometimes, acting as a counsellor and at other times as a critical friend, his insights and views could prove invaluable in times of change in life, as well as your career.

Mentors have to have much the same skills as coaches but their role is different. Mentors tend to be less proactive. They are people that are on hand to provide knowledge, guidance and insight on request. Their main role is to help you with your learning and personal development, either in the workplace or outside. They can explore with you how your behaviour and attitudes affect your performance at work and how you fit into the organisation. Sometimes, they may be referred to as buddies. Typically, they are experienced people with a high level of knowledge of the organisation and how things are done. You may find a mentor particularly useful at difficult times.

What to expect from a mentor

Mentors should always keep the subject matter confidential and it is important that you (the 'mentee') know that exchanges take place in confidence in a safe environment.

The mentor will support you in tackling the concerns and obstacles you are facing. He will use his knowledge and experience and provide practical and objective guidance and support to help you become the person you want to be. Here are some of the key aspects of mentoring:

» **Questioning and listening skills**

These should be used to help you reflect on your own performance, challenge your own assumptions, clarify your thinking and to identify situations where you need support in developing skills and knowledge.

» **Coming from the point of view of the learner (the jargon for this is 'learner-centredness')**

The mentor should suggest new ideas and different perspectives on the issues raised, at the same time as encouraging you to seek their own solutions.

» **Support, encouragement and counselling skills**

It is essential that he offers you support and encouragement. A mentor should use his counselling skills, but he should not take on the role of counsellor.

» **Feedback**

The mentor should provide honest feedback, praising or criticising your actions constructively, where needed, as a critical friend.

» **Staff development**

The mentor should offer you guidance on the skills you need to develop and how you can go about this.

» **Context**

If the mentor is from within your company, he should be able to bring to bear contextual information and knowledge about the company, its politics and informal networks.

» **Career plan**

The mentor should guide you into developing and managing a career plan and to support you in taking responsibility for your own personal development.

Mentoring supports all kinds of learning in that it can take place before or during training, or when you are carrying out your job. It gives you individual attention and immediate feedback.

Finding a mentor

» Your employer (if you have one) may provide a mentor in house to support your training and development. The company may have a mentoring scheme. This may be a line manager or other staff member, although it is good practice for the mentor to be someone who has no ongoing workplace relationship with you; for example, as a regular trainer or a line manager. That way the relationship is not complicated by other obligations.

» If you are considering external training, the training provider may offer mentoring as part of the package.

» You can shop around in your area. The contacts for coaching may help (see *Use a coach* on page 20), or contact the Mentoring and Befriending Foundation (see *Useful contacts* for its details). There may be a fee involved if you use a company or self-employed consultant, but there is a possibility that there may be a mentoring scheme in your area where you can find a mentor free of charge. For example, Business in the Community (see

Useful contacts for its details) exists to encourage businesses to have a positive impact on society, and it may help you find a mentor. Alternatively, your employer may help you with the fees, particularly if there is a benefit for the company.

» Ask around as you may be able to find a suitable person via friends or colleagues who could do this for you for free.

Unfortunately, anyone can, in theory, set themselves up as a mentor, so if you are going to pay a fee, you will need to carry out your own checks as to a mentor's qualifications and professional competence, and indeed whether you feel you can establish a fruitful relationship with him. Relying on a personal recommendation is best. Failing that, you can always ask for his customers' testimonials, and you should also be allowed to contact customers to see how they found his service.

Use a coach

This is a self-help book, but you may need assistance to help yourself and a coach can do this for you. The role of a coach is to facilitate the exploration of your needs, motivations, desires, skills and thought processes to assist you in making real, lasting change. A coach will provide informed support and guidance to help you develop as a person or to improve your skills and knowledge. There are two kinds of coach relevant here:

Skills coach

If you need help to develop your skills, you need a skills coach. This form of coaching is carried out on a one-to-one basis to develop your skills in the workplace. It is mostly used to support your learning on the job. Skills coaching programmes are tailored specifically to your needs, your knowledge, experience, maturity and ambitions and are generally focused on achieving a number of objectives for both you and the company. These objectives often include your being able to perform specific, well-defined tasks and they also take into account your personal and career development needs.

One-to-one skills training through coaching is not the same as the 'sitting next to Nelly' approach to on-the-job training. It is carried out by a professionally qualified or experienced person and is based on an assessment of your needs in relation to the job role. It is delivered in a structured (but highly flexible) manner, and generates measurable learning and performance outcomes. This form of skills training is likely to focus purely on the skills required to perform the job. However, it is important to know that coaches are facilitators, so instead of telling you what you should do, they will observe you in action to suggest new ideas at the same time as encouraging you to seek your own solutions. Usually, this work is centred on a specific activity. The outcomes include the following:

» **Achievement and growth**

You and the coach agree to complete challenging tasks which help you grow in confidence and competence, and keep you at the peak of your abilities.

» **Learning outcomes**

Your coach designs training events with learning outcomes in mind. He can help support you after an off-the-job training event to help ensure that you achieve the required outcome.

» **Standards**

Your coach can assist you to practise your skills so that you can achieve higher performance standards.

» **Practice**

Your coach can provide you with the opportunity to learn while you are doing something. Rather than just watching him, you can repeat skills using learning aids.

» **Correcting problems**

The close scrutiny and guidance of your coach can rectify your difficulties or bad habits.

» **Holistic training**

Your coach addresses your wider learning needs, rather than just specific skill areas.

There may be a number of staff in your workplace who could take on the role of coach, or at least have some coaching skills:

» **Managers**

For line managers and supervisors, coaching is integral to people management. Some managers will have difficulty in doing this (e.g. due to their workload or their staff being geographically widespread), but if they are serious about developing the skills of their staff, then they should coach.

» **Trainers**

They may need to coach you because specific on-the-job training may be required, or you may need additional assistance for a fixed time period following a particular training event. You may need coaching support with open or distance learning, or computer-based learning. The trainer should be experienced and preferably qualified in this area.

» **Other staff**

Coaching may also be carried out by other staff members; for example, a secretary could teach a manager keyboard skills.

» **Experienced staff**

They could be asked to coach you on specific skill areas (e.g. experienced staff could take on the equivalent of the 'master craftsman' role, which is undergoing a revival in the trades to provide guidance to new entrants on the job).

If your employer cannot provide you with a coach, there are two other options:

1. If you take up off-the-job training outside the workplace, see if the training provider can provide a coach to guide you in your work. This would be more effective if you could get your

employer's permission for the trainer to attend your workplace and guide you on the job.

2. You could contract a coach externally – see page 24 for contacts.

Life coach

A skills coach will help you develop your skills, but what can you do if you do not know what skills you want to develop? Can a coach help you improve your life to get the best out of the opportunities on offer? A life coach may be able to support you if:

» you do not have a clear idea of what you want to achieve;

» you do not have the time to think about what it is that you want as you are too busy trying to get through your daily to-do list before you collapse, exhausted, at the end of the day, having achieved little of lasting significance;

» you have harboured a dream for a career for a long time, but you never quite seem to get the time to think about it much, let alone do it. You are just too bogged down in your current job, or your other daily commitments.

Life coaching (or personal coaching) is growing significantly in the UK. Personal coaches may work face-to-face but email- and telephone-based relationships are also very common. A coach's role is to be highly supportive should you wish to make some form of significant change happen within your life.

A life coach will offer you a supportive and motivating environment so that you can explore what you want in life and how you may achieve your aspirations and fulfil your needs. He will work with you to examine your life as it is now and your life as you want it to be in the future, and he will then work on a way to bridge the gap.

By assisting you in committing to action and by being a sounding-board to your experiences, coaching allows you the personal space and support you need to grow and develop. Exciting things can happen when you focus, set yourself a goal and then work to achieve it. Energy seems to appear from nowhere, and making even the smallest change often leads to a domino effect so that, before you know it, powerful, positive shifts have happened in your life. Part of the coach's role is to assist you to maintain the motivation and commitment needed to achieve your goals once you know what they are.

In many cases life coaching is differentiated from skills coaching purely by the context and the focus of the programme. Skills coaching is always conducted within the constraints of the group you are part of, or the workplace context. Life coaching, on the other hand, is taken entirely from your own perspective.

Finding a coach

There are various sources of coaches:

» For skills coaching, your employer (if you have one) may provide a coach in house to support your training and development. This may be a line manager or other staff member.

» Again, for skills coaching, if you are considering external training, the training provider may offer coaching as part of the package.

» For both types of coaching, you can shop around in your area. Usually, this will be a company or self-employed consultant so you will have to pay his fees. With skills coaching, your employer may support you with the fees if it can see the benefit for the company. It may even consider supporting you with life coaching.

» You may also be able to find a coach at the Find a Life Coach website or from The Coaching Academy (see *Useful contacts* for details).

» Other professional coaching bodies or networks (which are not for profit and independent) are the Association for Coaching, the European Mentoring & Coaching Council, the International Coach Federation (ICF), and the Coaching & Mentoring Network. See *Useful contacts* for details.

Unfortunately, anyone can, in theory, set up as a coach, so you will need to carry out your own checks as to the coach's qualifications and professional competence, and indeed whether you feel that you can establish a fruitful relationship with him. The above organisations may help. If possible, get a personal recommendation. Failing that, ask the coach for customer testimonials and he should also allow you to contact his customers to see how they found his service.

Use a counsellor

The term 'counselling' is often associated with the giving of advice (e.g. careers counselling), but in this book I look at counselling in its professional context. It is defined as a set of skills used by a professionally qualified counsellor working with a client in a contractual counselling relationship.

Counselling involves someone actively listening to you. A counsellor should refrain from advising you, but he will enable you to reflect on your situation to help you draw your own conclusions. This process can help you to evaluate your strengths and weaknesses, and consider your opportunities for personal development. Counselling can help you to overcome your barriers to learning, by developing a change in your attitude or by helping you to resolve personal problems. It can also help you to feel less stressed in the workplace.

Alleviating workplace stress

In Britain statistics suggest that more than 40 million days are lost each year due to stress-related illnesses. Moreover, any form of training and development is likely to be rendered less effective if the learners are suffering from stress.

Stress is an individual reaction to events. It occurs when there is an imbalance between the demands made on the individual and his coping resources. In other words, what stresses one person may not stress another. The main reasons for this are individual differences: personality, motivation, the ability to cope with change, how events are perceived, the impact on the individual's values and beliefs, and the way he thinks about himself and his abilities. The effects of stress are also different for different people. It can affect thoughts, feelings and behaviour in different ways. However, whatever the causes and effects, as I have discussed elsewhere in this book, too much stress can have a radical influence on your motivation and ability to learn something new.

Counselling will help you understand more about what stresses you and what action you can take to try to alleviate the stress. It will help you learn more about yourself, and it will improve your psychological well-being. It may turn out that the main reason for your being under stress is something occurring in your personal life, although it could equally be work related. If it is the latter, you may need to raise the matter with your employer. Perhaps you are under stress because of the following reasons:

»   Difficult targets, poor supervision, insufficient opportunities for training and development, poor time management.

»   Your inability to do your job to the required standard.

»   Extenuating factors, such as harassment, bullying or discrimination.

»   Change or the fear of change, such as pending redundancies, downsizing or restructuring.

»   Your inability to relax away from work.

»   Your feeling unfulfilled in your work or personal life (or both).

Your employer now has a legal obligation, under health and safety legislation, to do all it can to alleviate workplace stress once it has been brought to its attention. This may include addressing organisational and management problems, as well as helping you to improve your ability to cope.

It is worth noting that your line manager or supervisor, and any trainer, coach or mentor available to you, should try to use his counselling skills to help you reflect on your learning. He should empower you by encouraging you to take ownership of your performance and training needs. For example, he should use his counselling skills at appraisals to ask questions such as, 'How do you feel you have performed this year?', 'Tell me what you think went well and not so well', 'How would you describe your communication skills?' Questions can also be used to encourage self-development, such as, 'What difficulties did you encounter?', 'What did you learn from these?' 'How can you apply this knowledge in the future?'

Test yourself

It is important to try to find a career that suits your personality and abilities. Psychometric tests are used by employers to help them make recruitment decisions, but undertaking one for your own benefit may help you. The tests are designed to assess your ability or personality in a measured and structured way. They may help you learn more about yourself, help you decide on your choice of occupation, or help you identify how you prefer to learn.

Careers specialists (see *Explore possible careers* on page 1) may be able to offer you a test or refer you to a specialist who will supervise you taking the test and analyse the results. A fee may be charged, but for this you will receive a professionally prepared analysis of your scores and a detailed report. A quick and simpler alternative would be to do an online test, although the results may be less accurate if you do not involve an expert. For information on the most reliable tests for your needs, contact the British Psychological Society or go to the Society's Psychological Testing Centre website (see *Useful contacts* for details). Online try Intraspec.ca (www.intraspec.ca/personality-tests.php), INTP.org (www.intp.org/tests) and Mind tools (www.mindtools.com/page12.html).

There is also a test called the Myers Briggs Analysis, devised by Isabel Meyers Briggs and Katherine Briggs, which allows you to analyse your personality type based on four different criteria. Humanmetrics.com allows you to complete this test and then it will automatically compute an online analysis for you. Log on to www.humanmetrics.com/cgi-win/JTypes1.htm.

Try a technique for faster learning

Learning may be conscious or unconscious, but everything we want to learn must always take a particular route – from ultra short-term memory to short-term memory, and then to long-term memory. In the physiological sense, learning is the transfer of information from the short-term to the long-term memory.

However, a lot of information does not get as far as the long-term memory at all. It has been estimated that 70 per cent of what you learn one day is forgotten by the following day, unless there is a deliberate attempt to consolidate the material in the long-term memory.

How can you speed up your learning?

» Repeat the same information or practise it several times. Repetition sets the memory mechanism in motion. Periodic review and practice will speed up learning.

» Associate information with rhymes or a rhythm (e.g. a piece of music). This helps learning because the brain is known to store information rhythmically.

» Try to relate your learning to a world with which you are familiar. For example, if you are training to be a manager or coach, you may want to reflect on how you have successfully organised or supported people in your personal life.

» Use different senses to absorb information. The more senses you are able to use, the faster and more efficiently you will learn. So if trainers can appeal to several senses simultaneously, the more effective they will be in teaching you.

» You will learn faster if you are highly motivated or are enjoying a training session. An emotional content to learning makes it easier to remember because you remember more in a higher state of arousal. This is because the movement of electrical impulses in the brain is speeded up by positive stress.

• You learn much more by 'doing' rather than just observing.

What slows down your learning?

» Too much, or too confusing, information has to be assimilated in too short a time. Training sessions which focus on providing as much information as possible in the shortest time span are rarely effective.

» Your means of absorbing information are too limited; for example, if you rely only on reading, you may only remember ten per cent (see table below).

» The brain sometimes pauses and bars receipt of new information due to overload. You should allow yourself time to take in new information and apply it, or to practise any new skills that you have learned.

» If you experience discomfort, distress or shock, this can block the electrical impulses to the long-term memory. Some people suffer more than others in situations that are potentially threatening, such as a performance test, role play, or having to do a presentation in front of colleagues.

Activity	We tend to remember	Our level of involvement
• Reading	10% of what we read	Verbal receiving
• Listening	20% of what we hear	Verbal receiving
• Looking at charts and diagrams • Watching a film or video	30% of what we see	Visual receiving
• Watching a demonstration or participating in a discussion	50% of what we both see and hear	Receiving and participating
• Making a presentation	70% of what we say	Participating
• Participating in a role play • Simulating or practising the real thing • Actually doing the real thing	80% of what we both say and do	Doing

Source: *The Use of Senses and Learning (adapted from Dale's 'Cone of Experience' (1954)*

The percentages in this chart are, of course, only averages, and factors discussed elsewhere in this book, such as motivation, perceived relevance of the training, the skill of the trainer, and whether the training matches the preferred learning styles of the participant, could all affect the data one way or another.

However, this chart shows that the more involved you are in learning, rather then just being a passive recipient, the more you are likely to learn and the faster you are likely to learn too.

Chapter 2

Learning in and out of the classroom

Inside the classroom

If you attend a classroom course, you will find that trainers and lecturers use a number of different training methods. To give you some awareness of the possibilities, this chapter lists some of the most common. Note that not all training is received in the classroom – see *Outside the classroom* on page 35 for details of the different methods that apply there.

If you want to get the maximum benefit from a course, you need to be trained using several of these methods. When you are choosing a course, it is worth finding out from the training provider what methods will be used so you can establish whether those on offer will suit your needs and whether there is sufficient variety. See Chapter 6 for information about the different kinds of training providers. Most of these methods will apply regardless of the subject matter, skill or career for which you are being trained.

Lecture or presentation

When most people think of training courses, they think of the lecture or presentation format. This is the most traditional. It is commonly associated with college and school. In this method, one person (the trainer) does most of the talking. He may use handouts, visual aids, questions and answers, or posters to support the lecture. It may be provided in your workplace, or you can attend an external course, such as one provided by a college or university.

The advantage of a lecture or presentation is that it provides a lot of information quickly in a short space of time. The disadvantage is that it does not actively involve you in the training process. You may not retain a lot of the information if it is only presented orally, so it is important for your learning that you also experience some of the other methods below.

» Workshop or syndicate

A workshop is generally a highly participative event, which brings together a number of individual learners who are developing particular skill areas. It is particularly useful for enabling you to come together with other people with different areas of interest and levels of experience to share your issues, as well as your good and bad experiences of doing your job. Through pooling your experience, you and the other participants can learn new approaches and skills.

A workshop is particularly useful in helping you if you are training to develop people skills, such as coaching, assertiveness, negotiation and facilitation. It allows these skills to be practised in a sheltered and supportive environment, and it provides you with the opportunity to give and receive feedback.

» Management development activity

Outdoor development is generally used to develop staff management skills; for example, team building, leadership skills, communication, planning and problem solving. You are usually asked to undertake some activity or series of activities where you have to rely on the resources of the group, and often this is outdoors (e.g. you have to get from A to B across the country, overcoming obstacles on the way).

These activities can provide a powerful learning environment if they are well structured and facilitated, with opportunities for debriefing and feedback. However, there may be some risk that the activities could expose tensions and conflicts between participants which, if unresolved, may then bubble up again in the workplace.

» Demonstration

A demonstration is very effective for basic skills training in numeracy and literacy (also known as Skills for Life – see Chapter 4 for more information). The trainer shows you how to do something and he then provides an opportunity for you to perform the task being demonstrated.

This method emphasises trainee involvement. It engages several senses – seeing, hearing, feeling and touching. However, it requires a great deal of trainer preparation and planning. There also needs to be an adequate space for the training to take place. If the trainer is not skilled in the task being taught, you may learn poor work habits.

» Seminar

A seminar often combines several group methods: lectures, discussions, conferences and demonstrations. The seminar room may be equipped with audio-visual PCs and other equipment in the classroom for you to practise on.

Group members are involved in the training. The trainer can use many group methods as part of the seminar activity. However, there is a big onus on the trainer to conduct the seminar properly, as more skill is required than with other methods. So if the trainer is not up to it, the seminar could go badly wrong.

» Conference

The conference training method is a good problem-solving approach. A group considers a specific problem or issue and it works to reach agreement on statements or solutions.

There is a lot of trainee participation and the trainer can use several methods (lecture, panel and seminar) to keep the sessions interesting. On the downside, opinions generated at the conference may differ from your manager's ideas, which may lead to confusion and conflict!

» **Panel**

The process invites you, and other employees, to share your opinions and you are then asked to seek alternatives to a situation. By being challenged you are more likely to reflect and think through your arguments, and you may learn more than with other methods. On the downside, if there are any organisational problems, things could get very chaotic and counter-productive!

» **Role play**

During a role play, you and your colleagues assume roles and act out certain situations. It is good for customer service and sales training.

You can learn the possible results of certain behaviours in a classroom situation. There is a good opportunity to practise people skills and you can experiment with many different approaches to a situation without alienating any actual customers.

However, a lot of time is spent making a single point. Trainers must be skilled and creative in helping the class learn from the situation. In some role play situations, only a few people get to practise while others watch.

» **Case study**

A case study is a description of a real or imagined situation which contains information that you can use to analyse what has occurred and why. You then recommend solutions based on the content provided.

This approach has the advantage of being flexible, allowing discussion on many aspects. However, it works best if the participants have already learned basic principles. Case studies are a good way of underpinning learning. On the downside, cases can be difficult to write and time-consuming to discuss. The trainer must be creative and very skilled at leading discussions, making points, and keeping trainees on track.

» **Simulation**

You participate in a reality-based, interactive activity where you imitate actions required on the job. It is a useful technique for skills development.

This method directly applies to jobs performed after training. Simulations involve different learning styles, increasing the chance that you will retain what you have learned. However, simulations are time-consuming. The trainer must be very skilled and make sure that you practise the skills correctly.

» **Films/videos/computer-based training**

Content for the training experience comes primarily from a videotape or computer-based program. It is easy to provide this training and the trainer can follow up with questions and a discussion. It is also easy to assure that the same information is presented to you and the other trainees. It is expensive to develop. Most trainers choosing this option must purchase the training from an outside vendor, making the content less specific to their needs.

Outside the classroom

You may have never been comfortable with traditional courses and examinations. Maybe you did not achieve too well at school, or perhaps you simply want a change. Whether or not this applies to you, learning outside the classroom gives you a new opportunity to learn and achieve qualifications. The following methods of learning outside the classroom mostly apply to workplace training.

» **Projects**

Projects require you to do something on the job which helps the company, as well as helping you to develop skills and learn about the topic. It may involve participation on a team, the creation of a database, or the forming of a new process. The type of project will vary depending on the type of business and your skill level.

This is a good training activity if you have some experience in the job. Projects can be chosen which help solve problems or otherwise improve the operation. You get first-hand experience in the topic of the training, and a chance to apply your ideas and learn from doing them. This method works best if your trainer or manager properly introduces the project and its purpose, your particular role, what outcomes are expected, and its relevance to the work of the company.

» ### Self-discovery

You discover competences on your own using techniques such as guided exercises, books and research. The advantage here is that you are able to choose the learning style that works best for you. You are able to move at your own pace and have a great deal of ownership over your learning. As with open learning (see page 43), it may be possible to fit it around your job commitments, although your employer should offer you some time off to do written work. You have more freedom of choice in your learning and you may be more motivated by being able to take responsibility for your learning in this way.

However, there is a risk that you could easily get side-tracked and you may learn slowly. It may also be more difficult for you to measure your own progress.

» ### Self-directed learning

This method may lead to some training both in and out of the classroom. The key here is that you are responsible for the management of your training and the updating of your career with some help from trainers, coaches or line managers. This approach is similar to open learning and fits in with the concept of lifelong learning and Continuing Professional Development (see the Introduction, *Test the employer* on page xxi).

Questionnaires or pre-tests may be used to enable you to assess your present knowledge, skills or attitudes in a particular area; for example, supervisory skills, communication skills and equal opportunities awareness. This will help you to clarify your learning objectives and enable trainers to design a relevant training package with you. You could be asked to provide information prior to the start of a training event that could be used as course material (e.g. problem situations and difficulties you have experienced). You could also be asked to set out your expectations and needs in advance of the training. Of course, some of this information may already have been collected as part of an appraisal or training needs assessment, but asking for this additional data will help the trainers provide you with an opportunity to shape the course content.

You may be offered opportunities to qualify for National Vocational Qualifications (NVQs) or Open College Network (OCN) credits. The use of this approach may offer you more choice on how you can address your learning needs than traditional training courses.

» Learning contract

Some employers may want to set out a learning contract – a three-way agreement between you, the company (usually represented as your line manager or supervisor) and the training staff. This will enable training to be organised to suit your needs and those of your employer. This may be training in or out of the classroom. The contract may set out:

» what training needs to be done (this could have been arrived at from appraisals or other training needs surveys);

» how it is to be done;

» by when;

» the resources required to facilitate its success; and

» what evidence is required to show that the learning outcomes have been achieved.

The negotiation of a contract is the key activity to preventing problems that you may have in studying and should be undertaken before any training intervention begins. It is an initial opportunity to start forming a relationship of respect and trust between you and the trainer.

» **Self-development**

This method requires you to take responsibility for your own development, but it can only work effectively if it is complemented by some of the methods in this list, and if you are adequately supported. This method is best achieved by means of on-the-job training, such as coaching or mentoring, one-to-one supervision sessions or appraisals where goals are identified and negotiated and organisational resources are made available by way of support.

This method is sometimes seized on by organisations that want to reduce the training budget as part of a cost-saving exercise, as they see it as a cheap option. But if it is to be carried out effectively, time and resources must be expended.

» **On-the-job training**

On-the-job training (OJT) is an activity undertaken at the workplace which is designed to improve your skills or knowledge. It is usually a planned and structured activity which is delivered on a one-to-one basis.

Many of the advantages of OJT are the same as for open learning, but with OJT training can be delivered at the optimum time; for example, immediately before a job is to be performed 'for real' in the workplace. You will have opportunities to practise immediately, and you are likely to have immediate feedback. Also, usually the training is delivered by colleagues and this can help integrate you into a team.

The disadvantage of using OJT is that there may be a tendency for it to be fitted in when it is convenient for office routine rather than you as a learner. There is a risk that the training may be given piecemeal and may not be properly planned, and you may gain a fragmented picture of the company. Alternatively, too much training may be delivered in one session leading to 'information overload' which you could find tiring and counter-productive. For it to work well, a lot of planning and commitment from the company is required, using trainers who are skilled coaches. Immediate practice should follow, accompanied by feedback so you attain the maximum benefit.

» ## Competence-based learning

In the UK the Qualifications and Curriculum Authority (QCA) (See *Useful contacts* for details) defines competence as 'the ability to perform in work roles or jobs to the standard required in employment'. The National Vocational Qualification (NVQ) system is one example of the competence-based approach. Another is the Open College Network system (see page 45).

Explicit standards and statements of performance are defined by each industry and your performance is measured against these specific criteria or standards, rather than with someone else. You either meet the standard and pass, or you fail and need additional training and re-assessing.

Competence-based learning is centred around your learning needs, providing individualised learning plans and assessments of your performance or training needs, and learning on the job. The approach represents a good example of self-directed learning.

The advantage of this method is that it gives you a clearer focus on what you need to do to develop and improve your performance. Also, the training can be flexible. You can work towards your qualification as part of your normal job, or at college, through open learning or private study, or through a combination of these methods. You can also proceed at your own pace, rather than having to keep up with the rest of the group. Indeed, if you can provide evidence that you have existing knowledge, skills or experience in the field, you can gain exemption from certain elements; for example, if you can show that you have experience of interviewing staff, you may be able to skip a training module on interviewing skills. This is called Accreditation of Prior Learning – see the QCA's website for more information.

The following methods could apply to workplace training, but they do not have to. They could apply to you in any situation.

» *National Vocational Qualifications (NVQs)*

NVQs are 'competence-based' qualifications. If you do not like the idea of classroom study or exams, an NVQ may appeal to you. You learn practical, work-related tasks designed to help you develop the skills and knowledge you need to do a job effectively. They are based on national standards for occupations (see Chapter 3, *Occupational standards* on page 61). There are NVQs for almost all of the occupations. The standards say what a competent person in a job should be expected to do. As you progress through the course, you compare your skills and knowledge with these standards as you learn, so you can see what you need to do to meet them.

NVQs are at levels 1 to 5 on the National Qualifications Framework. They are available to you whatever your age or stage of your career. There are no formal entry requirements, although the higher levels need more experience in the occupation. Within reason, this means that you can decide the pace, place and way in which you want to learn.

NVQs are broken down into units which are achieved through assessment and training. You attain an NVQ by demonstrating to an assessor that you can actually do a job in practice, to the national standards required. Assessment is normally through on-the-job observation and questioning. You will also have to collect evidence to prove that you have the skills and knowledge to achieve each unit and to meet the standards you are studying for.

The standards are developed by Standards Setting Bodies, and then formed into qualifications by awarding bodies which are accredited by the National Council for Vocational Qualifications (NCVQ). These awarding bodies register assessment centres at local and national level to provide NVQ services to organisations. Once approved, standards are kept under review and their 'product life' is limited to three to five years. The overseeing bodies are the

QCA or the Scottish Qualifications Authority (SQA). The five levels of NVQs are:

Level 1: Foundation skills in occupations – work activities which are routine and predictable.

Level 2: Operative or semi-skilled occupations – activities which are complex or non-routine, with some individual responsibility or autonomy, and teamwork.

Level 3: Technician, craft, skilled and supervisory occupations – activities which are complex and non-routine, with considerable responsibility, autonomy and control, or guidance of others.

Level 4: Technical and junior management occupations – activities with a substantial degree of personal responsibility and autonomy. Responsibility for the work of others and the allocation of resources is often present.

Level 5: Chartered, professional and senior management occupations – activities with very substantial personal autonomy and often significant responsibility for the work of others, and for the allocation of substantial resources. There is also personal responsibility for analysis, diagnosis, design, planning, execution and evaluation.

Scottish Vocational Qualifications (SVQs), the Scottish equivalent of NVQs, are awarded at five levels – SVQ 1 (SCQF level 4), SVQ 2 (SCQF level 5), SVQ 3 (SCQF level 6), SVQ 4 (SCQF level 8) and SVQ 5 (SCQF level 11) – see Chapter 3 for more information. They are accredited by the SQA and are offered by a range of awarding bodies.

» *Scottish Progression Awards (SPAs)*

These are designed to provide some of the skills, knowledge and understanding required for a related SVQ. They are normally subsets of SVQs and they offer you an opportunity to achieve a group of units which encourages progression to a full SVQ. SPAs can comprise a group of SVQ Units, a group of National or Higher National Units, or a combination of these.

HELP AND ADVICE

Contact your local Further Education College or, if you are working, talk to your employer or your company's human resources department, if it has one. If it offers NVQ-based training, it should have a contract with an awarding body specific to your occupation. It should also have a contract with an Assessment and Accreditation Centre (AAC) or an Assessment, Delivery and Accreditation Centre (ADAC), unless it is registered to become a centre itself, which it may be if it trains a lot of people at one time. The QCA website has information on NVQs and how they can be achieved. If you are under 19, contact Connexions, plus the BBC Radio 1 Onelife website has information (www.bbc.co.uk/radio1/onelife).

» Distance learning

These courses can be studied without your having to go into a classroom. All of your course materials are sent to you and many courses will even be assessed without your going in for an exam. The course materials may include traditional correspondence courses, online courses and interactive CD-roms, open learning centres and face-to-face training, which allows time for self-study and learning support.

With this method you mostly work at your own pace and fix your own deadlines. While this may appeal to you, it also brings its own challenges in that you will have to be motivated and self-disciplined. Although you may want the qualification, will you want to study in the evenings if you have been at work all day? You will also have to set yourself targets and stick to them.

Distance learning may suit you if your work or domestic schedule is irregular and you cannot commit to a course at a certain time each week; for example, due to childcare or erratic work patterns. It may also suit you if you did not like school and the whole classroom experience, but not if you are the type of person who likes the support of other learners.

Also, the method is more appropriate for learning technical skills or knowledge (e.g. computer skills). The learning of practical skills, such as midwifery or driving a fork-lift truck, could not be done at home!

There are a few providers that offer a large range of subjects – academic courses (such as GCSEs), vocational courses (such as computing), professional courses (such as banking), and leisure courses you may study for pleasure (such as painting). The best known is the National Extension College or Learn Direct (see *Useful contacts* for details).

» Flexible learning

Flexible learning, sometimes referred to as 'blended learning', involves a combination of the out-of-classroom methods (listed in this chapter), carefully put together by the trainer to suit your needs, and the requirements of the subject. It is similar to distance learning in that you usually work at your own pace, and quite often it can incorporate open learning and e-learning.

A series of learning resources are provided which are either paper-based or in the form of interactive computer software, and you are given feedback through assessment. Usually, there is support from a tutor or a line manager who you may meet from time to time, or who may support you on the telephone or online. You may be able to attend workshops at certain times. Various tasks are completed and assessed and, depending on the subject and the training institution, there may be a formal examination at the end of the programme of work. In order to find out more, contact the training institution (the college, university or other provider) for the subject you wish to study.

» Open learning

Open learning is so called because it is open to anyone. It is a kind of distance or flexible learning which you can take up whether or not you have any other qualifications. There are some entry requirements for certain courses, but the good news is that these can be achieved by doing a prerequisite course, and in many cases this will count towards the later qualification if you go on to do it.

It is often based on real-life work situations, so that you can use resources other than the trainer to facilitate your learning, such as line managers, colleagues, mentors or coaches. In order to keep track of your progress, there is a lot of emphasis on assessment, including self-assessment. This will help you to keep track of what you have learned and to apply it in your job, if you are learning in connection with your employment. Open learning fits well with an accreditation; for example, you can work towards an NVQ or Open College Network modules.

It may be possible to fit your learning around your job commitments, although your employer should offer you some time off to do written work. With open learning, you have more freedom of choice in your learning. A menu of training is made available, but in consultation with your line managers and trainer, you may be able to decide in what order to select modules, or indeed whether to skip modules altogether, if you can show that you already have the skills and knowledge. You may be more motivated by being able to take responsibility for your learning in this way. The advantage of traditional training courses is not lost. The options on offer should include a fair proportion of courses, workshops or other delivery formats.

The more commonly known large course providers are the Open University and the National Open College Network (NOCN). Some course providers specialise in certain types of courses; for example, the Open College of the Arts offers a range of art and design courses. See *Useful contacts* for details.

» *The Open University*

With the Open University you can study at higher education and postgraduate education level. Nearly all study part time, and about 70 per cent of undergraduate students are in full-time employment. You could ask your employer, if you have one, to see if it would be prepared to sponsor you. With most courses there are no previous qualifications required to study. You have to be aged 18 when your course starts but there is no upper age limit.

» *The National Open College Network*

National Open College Network (NOCN) courses are designed to further your development by leading to off-the-peg qualifications in a wide range of subjects and areas, including Skills for Life and entry level qualifications (see Chapter 4). Also, they can work with employers at local level to design tailor-made in-house learning programmes to suit the needs of the company and the employees. Quite often a 'pick 'n' mix' approach might be best, where both these options are taken up in combination to meet the needs of the workplace and yourself. Most NOCN courses are a mixture of classroom-based and practical work-related activities. There are 11 Open College Networks (OCNs) in England, Wales and Northern Ireland, overseen by the NOCN – for information on their whereabouts, log on to the NOCN website (see *Useful contacts* for details).

An OCN Certificate is awarded if you can show learning achievement. You will have to successfully complete a number of units to achieve an OCN Certificate. A unit is a set of learning outcomes. You are awarded a credit on the successful completion of a unit, once assessment procedures have been followed. A credit is awarded for the achievement of those outcomes which a learner, on average, might reasonably be expected to achieve in a notional 30 hours of learning. Within the credit framework there are four set levels: entry level, level 1 (equivalent to NVQ level 1, GNVQ foundation level and the attainment of D to G grade at GCSE level), level 2 (equivalent to NVQ level 2, and the attainment of A* to C grade at GCSE level) and level 3 (equivalent to NVQ level 3, or GCE A-level).

HELP AND ADVICE

Talk to your employer or your company's human resources department, if it has one. If it offers OCN-based training, it should have a contract with the regional OCN. The company itself may be registered as an OCN approved training body, if it trains a lot of people at one time.

» E-learning

E-learning can be CD-rom-based, network-based, intranet-based or internet-based. Its quality, as in every form of training, is in its content and its delivery. This form of learning can suffer from many of the same pitfalls as classroom training, such as boring slides, monotonous speeches and little opportunity for interaction. Although, on the positive side, new software is always becoming available, much of it innovative and exciting in its potential.

E-learning falls into four categories, from the very basic to the very advanced. The categories are:

1. **Knowledge databases:** While they are not necessarily seen as actual training, these databases are the most basic form of e-learning. They can be specific sites that allow you to download articles or tools. These are usually moderately interactive, meaning that you can either type in a keyword or phrase to search the database, or make a selection from an alphabetical list.

2. **Online support:** This comes in the form of forums, chatrooms, online bulletin boards, email, or live instant messaging support. Slightly more interactive than knowledge databases, online support offers the opportunity for more specific questions and answers, as well as more immediate answers.

3. **Asynchronous training:** This is e-learning in the more traditional sense of the word. It involves self-paced learning delivered off the computer hard drive, or via a CD-rom with audio and video capabilities or it can be network-based, intranet-based or internet-based. Alternatively, it may be totally self-contained with links to reference materials in place of a live instructor. Online learning portals link to particular resources available on the

internet, and in some cases it may include access to instructors or facilitate online learning communities; for example, by providing message boards, online discussion groups and email. You may be able to take up this method in a small group or on your own.

4. **Synchronous training:** This occurs in real time with a live instructor facilitating the training. Everyone logs in at a set time and they can then communicate directly with the instructor and with each other. It lasts for a set amount of time – from a single session to several weeks, months or even years. This type of training usually takes place via internet websites, audio or video conferencing, internet telephony, or even two-way live broadcasts to students in a classroom.

If courses are planned and designed well, e-learning can make learning fun and interesting, as it uses a range of images, sounds and text, as well as games and quizzes. There is also potential for interaction with other e-learners and an e-instructor by means of chatrooms, discussion boards, instant messaging and email. E-learning courses can also build in immediate feedback to correct misunderstood material.

You are able to go through the course at your own pace. Courses offer user-controlled elements that just are not feasible in regular training classes. For example, with medical training, you can differentiate the sound of an irregular heartbeat from that of a regular heartbeat by clicking on icons on the screen and this allows you to listen at your own pace and replay the sound as often as you like.

A disadvantage of e-learning is that it can be a solitary pursuit and it will not suit you if you like to train with other people. However, it can be blended with other training to mitigate this; for example, with coaching to ensure on-the-job application, and workshops to allow you to discuss your learning and its applications face to face.

A major provider of e-learning is Learn Direct (see Chapter 6)

Checklist on good training

To help you judge the effectiveness of a training event, take a look through the checklist below. If the majority of points on the list have been met, then the training quality is likely to be good.

Training need

☐ Was a training need identified to justify participation?

☐ Was more than one method of identifying your training needs used?

Learning skills

☐ Were your current learning skills established so that appropriate training could be provided to meet your needs; for example, were your strengths and weaknesses identified?

On-the-job learning

☐ Were on-the-job learning or competence-based learning options considered?

☐ Was learning from experience encouraged?

☐ Was coaching made available to you?

Differences between learners

☐ If learners with different abilities or levels of competence were booked into the same training event, were steps taken to ensure that the training objectives and outcomes met with all their needs, including yours (perhaps by dividing them into separate groups, or supporting them as individuals)?

Physical obstacles to learning

☐ Has any attempt been made to deal with any factors which might impede learning for you; for example, if you have hearing loss, have arrangements been made to cater for this, such as the provision of a signer?

Clarifying expectations

- ☐ Were you given information at the start on what would be expected of you; for example, topics to be dealt with, the learning objectives, what activities you will be involved in (group discussion, role plays, listening to presentations, etc.)?

Previous knowledge, skills and experience

- ☐ Was your previous experience taken into account?
- ☐ Were your existing skills, knowledge and understanding (i.e. your current competence) taken into account?

Your attitudes and expectations

- ☐ Were your attitudes to the subject taken into account?
- ☐ Were your expectations discussed and taken on board?
- ☐ Were any of your fears or anxieties, if you had any, elicited and if so, were they alleviated?
- ☐ Was your motivation for undergoing the training established?
- ☐ Was it established whether the training was the answer for you in this case? (In some situations training may not be the answer, or it may only tackle the symptoms and the root of the problem may be to do with the way the organisation is run, or you may not need the training at that particular time.)

Training

- ☐ Were your training objectives identified and explained?
- ☐ Were they met?
- ☐ Were there opportunities for discussion and individual contribution?
- ☐ Was the person responsible for delivery effective in his role?
- ☐ Was training delivered at the most appropriate time, with breaks timed at appropriate intervals?

☐ In the case of training away from the workplace, were arrangements for booking the training satisfactory, as well as the venue, refreshments and other facilities?

☐ Was the level of content appropriate, together with the delivery methods and the resources available?

☐ Could anything have been added to the training intervention, or was anything regarded as unnecessary?

Evaluation

☐ Have attempts been made to ensure that the learners are satisfied with all aspects of the training intervention? (In the case of a course consisting of several units a mini-questionnaire may be used at the end of every unit followed by a larger one at the end.)

☐ In order to get more sophisticated responses, did some questions ask participants to score their replies (e.g. by using a scale of 1 to 6) and did they ask for their comments?

Chapter 3

Climbing the qualifications ladder

Qualification standards

When you choose to study, you may want to know how the standard of a qualification compares to others. You may also want to find out whether it can lead to further qualifications and if there is a 'ladder' you can climb to get better qualified.

In England, Northern Ireland and Wales the National Qualifications Framework (NQF) and the Framework for Higher Education Qualifications (FHEQ) have been developed to set out the levels of different qualifications. The equivalent in Scotland is the Scottish Credit and Qualifications Framework (SCQF).

The National Qualifications Framework

Set out below are the eight NQF levels, with examples of qualifications at each level. Note that the framework does not cover all the qualifications in existence; only those that have been accredited by the regulators. The ones that are included are approved as being of high quality, and meet the needs of learners and employers. Other qualifications will be added to the framework over time. Some qualifications span more than one level; for example, BTEC National Diplomas or National Vocational Qualifications (NVQs).

Within any one level, qualifications can cover a wide mix of subjects and take different amounts of time to complete. The information on entry requirements is only guidance; if you do not meet these requirements, it is always worth asking for an interview with the training provider, college, university or other institution because they may be flexible. This may particularly be likely if you have some paid or voluntary work experience in the subject area, or in a related area.

All the qualifications outlined below are discussed more fully in Chapter 4.

» **NQF entry level**

Examples of qualifications:

 » Entry level certificates.

 » Skills for Life at entry level.

What they give you:

 » Basic knowledge and skills.

 » The ability to apply learning in everyday situations.

 » They are not geared towards specific occupations.

Entry requirements: None.

» **NQF level 1**

Examples of qualifications:

 » GCSE grades D to G.

 » NVQs.

 » BTEC Introductory Diplomas and Certificates.

 » OCR Nationals.

 » Key Skills level 1.

 » Skills for Life.

What they give you:

 » Basic knowledge and skills.

 » The ability to apply learning with guidance or supervision.

» They may be linked to job competence.

Entry requirements: None.

» NQF level 2

Examples of qualifications:

» GCSE grades A* to C.

» NVQs.

» BTEC First Diplomas and Certificates.

» OCR Nationals.

» Key Skills level 2.

» Skills for Life.

What they give you:

» Good knowledge and understanding of a subject.

» The ability to perform a variety of tasks with some guidance or supervision.

» They may be appropriate for many job roles. For examples, see Chapter 9.

Entry requirements: If you want to study for a level 2 BTEC and OCR National qualification, you will generally need GCSE grades D to G, or a level 1 qualification in a similar subject.

» NQF level 3

Examples of qualifications:

» A-levels.

» Advanced Extension Awards.

» GCE in applied subjects.

» International Baccalaureate.

» Key Skills level 3.

» NVQs.

» BTEC Diplomas, Certificates and Awards.

» BTEC Nationals.

» OCR Nationals.

What they give you:

» The ability to gain or apply a range of knowledge, skills and understanding, at a detailed level.

» They may be appropriate if you plan to go to university, work independently or (in some cases) supervise and train others in their field of work.

Entry requirements: To study a level 3 BTEC and OCR Nationals qualification, you will normally need GCSE grades A*to C, or a level 2 qualification in a related subject. In some cases, if you want to take a level 3 course, such as an A-level, you will be expected to have a GCSE at grade B or above in the same subject.

Some schools and colleges also ask that you have GCSE grade C or above in English and Maths. If you are a mature student, the college may be more flexible about entry requirements.

» **NQF level 4**

Examples of qualifications:

» Key Skills level 4.

» NVQs.

» BTEC Professional Diplomas, Certificates and Awards, including Higher National Certificates (HNCs).

What they give you:

» Specialist learning, involving detailed analysis of a high level of information and knowledge in an area of work or study.

» They may be appropriate for people working in technical and professional jobs, and/or managing and developing others.

Entry requirements: For a BTEC Professional Diploma, you would be expected to have at least a Higher National Certificate in any subject (UK), or a BTEC Certificate, or two GCE A-levels.

You may be expected to have studied the same or a similar subject at a lower level. For the NVQ you may be expected to have completed level 3. Sometimes, if you have a period of relevant work experience, you may be able to enter without some of these qualifications.

» **NQF level 5**

Examples of qualifications:

» NVQs.

» BTEC Professional Diplomas, Certificates and Awards including Higher National Diplomas (HNDs).

What they give you:

» The ability to increase the depth of knowledge and understanding of an area of work or study, so you can respond to complex problems and situations.

» They involve a high level of work expertise and competence in managing and training others.

» They may be appropriate for people working as higher grade technicians, professionals or managers.

Entry requirements: Most HND courses require at least one A-level (or equivalent level 3 qualification). For the NVQ you may be expected to have completed level 4. Sometimes, if you have a period of relevant work experience, you may be able to enter without some of these qualifications.

» **NQF level 6**

Examples of qualifications:

» National Diploma in Professional Production Skills.

» BTEC Advanced Professional Diplomas, Certificates and Awards.

What they give you:

» A specialist, high-level knowledge of an area of work or study, to enable you to use your own ideas and research in response to complex problems and situations.

» They may be appropriate for people working as knowledge-based professionals or in professional management positions.

Entry requirements: Usually, you will be expected to be working in the field. Qualifications at levels 4 or 5 may be required, although this requirement may be waived if you are experienced in the subject.

» NQF level 7

Examples of qualifications:

» Diploma in Translation.

» BTEC Advanced Professional Diplomas, Certificates and Awards.

What they give you:

» Highly developed and complex levels of knowledge, enabling you to develop original responses to complicated and unpredictable problems and situations.

» They may be appropriate for senior professionals and managers.

Entry requirements: Usually, you will be expected to be working in the field. Qualifications at levels 4 to 6 may be required, although this requirement may be waived if you are experienced in the subject.

» NQF level 8

Examples of qualifications:

» Specialist awards.

What they give you:

» An opportunity to develop new and creative approaches that extend or redefine existing knowledge or professional practice.

» They may be appropriate for leading experts or practitioners in a particular field.

Entry requirements: Usually, you will be expected to be working in the field. Qualifications at levels 4 to 7 may be required, although this requirement may be waived if you are experienced in the subject.

You can find out more about the NQF at the Qualifications and Curriculum Authority's (QCA) website (see *Useful contacts* for details).

Vocational qualifications

Vocational qualifications provide you with the skills and education that prepare you for a particular job. Vocational qualifications can range from general qualifications, where you learn skills relevant to a variety of jobs, to specialist qualifications designed for a particular sector. There are many to choose from. They are available from several awarding bodies, such as City & Guilds, Edexcel and OCR Examinations, and can be taken at many different sizes and levels. A wide range of vocational qualifications are accredited into the NQF. These cover almost every industry sector, and every level of the NQF. Consequently, they vary in terms of size, level and assessment arrangements, ranging from broad-based to specialist qualifications designed for a particular sector. In many cases qualifications at several levels are available, enabling you to progress through the levels of the NQF.

In order to make it easier for you to know which level a qualification is pitched at, the QCA has asked English awarding bodies to standardise the titles of accredited vocational qualifications. The table below sets out the levels of various titles. However, it is important to double-check with the awarding body from its literature or website, or by asking the organisation.

Qualification titles	NQF level
Advanced Certificate/ Certificate (level 3)/ Diploma (level 3)	3 Advanced level
Intermediate Certificate/ Certificate (level 2)	2 Intermediate level
Foundation Certificate/ Certificate (level 1)	1 Foundation level

The Framework for Higher Education Qualifications

The Framework for Higher Education Qualifications (FHEQ) has been designed by the higher education sector and it contains descriptions of all the main higher education qualifications. It applies to degrees, diplomas, certificates and other academic awards granted by a university or higher education college.

The FHEQ broadly corresponds with levels 4 to 8 of the NQF, in terms of the demands the qualifications place on learners.

FHEQ level	Examples of qualifications
Certificate	· Certificates of higher education
Intermediate	· Foundation degrees · Ordinary (bachelor's) degrees · Diplomas of higher education and further education · Higher National Diplomas · Other higher diplomas
Honours	· Bachelor's degrees with honours · Graduate certificates and graduate diplomas
Masters	· Master's degrees · Postgraduate certificates · Postgraduate diplomas
Doctoral	· Doctorates

You can find out more about the FHEQ at the Quality Assurance Agency for Higher Education's website (see *Useful contacts* for details).

The exact qualifications and grades needed for different higher education courses vary widely. In general, though, you can apply to do a higher education course with:

» academic qualifications (such as A-levels or the International Baccalaureate);

» vocational qualifications (such as NVQs or BTEC National Diplomas and Certificates);

» foundation or access course qualifications.

If you already have a particular full-time higher education course in mind, you can look up the entry requirements on the UCAS website (see *Useful contacts* for details).

Scottish Credit and Qualifications Framework

The Scottish Credit and Qualifications Framework (SCQF) has been created by bringing together all mainstream Scottish qualifications into a single unified framework – that is, higher education qualifications, including HNCs and HNDs and National Qualifications such as Highers and Advanced Highers and Scottish Vocational Qualifications (SVQs). The framework covers all levels from Access 1 (National Qualification) to HE Doctorate (see the table on the following page for the 12 levels). At the time of writing, discussions are taking place to bring other Scottish qualifications, including those of professional and statutory bodies, into the framework.

The SCQF was developed and is being established jointly by the organisations in Scotland that have prime responsibility for qualifications. These are the Scottish Qualifications Authority (SQA), the Scottish Executive, the Quality Assurance Agency for Higher Education Scottish Office (QAA) and Universities Scotland.

SCQF levels are not directly related to years of study. In some circumstances, all or most of the study undertaken in a year will be at one level and progression will be from level to level. However, this is not a requirement of the SCQF. In many programmes students are likely to undertake courses at different levels in the framework. During a lifetime of learning, individuals will often move from a higher to a lower level qualification as they take on new learning and acquire new skills.

The Scottish Credit and Qualifications Framework

SCQF level	The Scottish Credit SQA National Units, Courses and Group Awards	Higher education	Framework SVQ*	SCQF Level
12		Doctorates		12
11		Masters	SVQ 5	11
10		Honours degree Graduate Diploma/Certificate		10
9		Ordinary degree Graduate Diploma/Certificate		9
8		Higher National Diploma Diploma in H. Ed.	SVQ 4	8
7	Advanced Higher	Higher National Certificate Certificate in H. Ed.		7
6	Higher		SVQ 3*	6
5	Intermediate 2 Credit Standard Grade		SVQ 2	5
4	Intermediate 1 General Standard Grade		SVQ 1	4
3	Access 3 Foundation Standard Grade			3
2	Access 2			2
1	Access 1			1

* The positioning of SVQs in the table gives a broad indication of their place in the framework. However, their place is still under review to ensure consistency with England and Wales, so some changes may be made later. Also note that often SVQs are made up of units at a number of levels – contact the SQA for further information.

All qualifications awarded or accredited by SQA and all qualifications awarded by Scottish degree-awarding institutions will be placed on the levels of the SCQF. Smaller components of qualifications (such as SQA units or university modules) will be allocated to a single level. This will be done progressively over the next few years. Larger qualifications that are made up of a number of components (e.g. group awards) will be allocated a final or exit level, but will often be composed of components at a number of different levels. For example, a student who completes a Scottish Group Award will normally have completed units at two levels, while a holder of an Honours degree will normally have completed courses and/or modules at four levels.

Occupational standards

In order to help you identify your training needs, it is worth checking to see if there are any National Occupational Standards (NOS) for your job.

These are statements of performance standards that describe what competent people in a particular occupation are expected to be able to do. They cover all the main aspects of an occupation, including current best practice, the ability to adapt to future requirements, and the knowledge and understanding which underpins competent performance.

If there are NOS for your job, or the job you are aiming for, then you can work out where the gaps in your skills are and have a clear idea of the training you need. A benefit of occupational standards is that they provide opportunities for you to obtain NVQs as they are designed to complement the NVQ Framework (or SVQs in Scotland).

Standards have been devised for many occupations in the UK and the plan is eventually to have them in place for every occupation in the country. The standards are developed by standards setting bodies. Membership of these bodies comprises representatives from the public sector, industry, professional bodies, employers, trade associations and practitioners. Further information about how standards are developed can be obtained from the QCA or the SQA (see *Useful contacts* for details). The Skills for Business website has a directory where you can search for occupational standards relevant to your needs. Log on to www.ukstandards.org.

The standards allow trainers to identify the current competence of individuals or a group of staff against a set of clearly defined standards for their particular occupational area. This means that a design brief for particular training can be put together with much more precision and it can then be easily agreed on what training is required, as the standards are set and cannot be deviated from. This, in turn, will aid the evaluation process.

Although there are variations from one standards setting body to the other, and some standards will be much more complex than others, a common format is based on the following:

» **Key roles**

These are the general areas of responsibility within an occupation (e.g. for a manager, one key role is 'managing finance').

» **Units**

Each key role contains a number of units (e.g. for a manager one unit would be 'monitor and control the use of resources').

» **Elements**

Each unit contains a number of elements (e.g. 'monitor and control activities against budgets' would be one element of the above unit).

» **Performance criteria**

These set out details on how the elements are to be achieved (taking the above example, one performance criteria would be 'requests for expenditure outside the manager's responsibility are promptly referred to the appropriate people').

» **Range indicators**

This relates to the variations that occur within an occupation (so, taking the above example, one range indicator may be 'monitoring relates to an accounting centre for which the manager has responsibility').

Once standards have been developed and approved by the standards setting body they are formed into qualifications by awarding bodies which are accredited by the National Council for Vocational Qualifications to form NVQs or SVQs. In Chapter 9 there is a list of occupations for which standards exist, together with the appropriate standards setting body you should contact for further information.

Help and advice

If you are interested in gaining a qualification, choosing from the huge range available can seem daunting. But do not panic; there is a lot of help and advice to assist you to pick a qualification that is right for you.

If you are at school, talk to your careers adviser or form tutor and if you are under 19, you can contact Connexions. Its jobs4u career database (see www.connexions-direct.com/jobs4u) will give you an idea of the type of qualifications, skills, working hours and salary associated with each job.

If you are any age, contact Learn Direct (see *Useful contacts* for details). It provides advice from its websites and telephone helplines, and it also has over a million courses. The advice available is wide ranging, such as how to access workplace learning, or training schemes if you are unemployed. It also tells you about training if you have no qualifications, how to return to learning, how to develop computer skills, how to retrain, and explains further and higher education. It also discusses flexible learning, how to obtain childcare while studying, and how you can finance your learning.

The Department for Children, Schools and Families website (www.lifelonglearning.co.uk) also provides information on all areas of education and learning, as does the government's central website (www.direct.gov.uk). The BBC website (www.bbc.co.uk/learning) has advice for 16–24-year olds and adults alike. The site contains over half a million pages of news, entertainment and factual material. Also, take a look at the Aimhigher and Open University websites (see *Useful contacts* for details) to get an idea of the type of course you can do, how long it takes to complete and what it costs.

There is a UK qualifications database at the website of the UK National Reference Point for Vocational Qualifications at www.uknrp.org.uk.

Finally, friends, parents or carers may also be able to offer you advice and support to help you make your decision.

Finding out more about qualifications

You can find out more about all qualifications from the awarding bodies (see below) or you can search for an accredited qualification on the website of the National Database of Accredited Qualifications (NDAQ). Scottish qualifications can be searched for on the SQA. See *Useful contacts* for both of the organisations' details. For more information on what sort of careers and jobs would be advanced by vocational qualifications, see Chapter 9.

There are over 100 awarding bodies offering QCA-accredited programmes in England. These range greatly in terms of the quantity of programmes provided and the number of students completing the qualifications. The following awarding bodies represent the largest organisations and those that offer their own vocational qualifications in tandem with national awards. They are:

» **Edexcel Foundation**

Its specialist vocational qualifications cover the BTEC structure of BTEC Firsts, Nationals and Higher Nationals. For more detailed information about these awards, please consult the Edexcel website (see *Useful contacts* for details).

» **The Assessment and Qualifications Authority (AQA)**

AQA is the largest of the English exam boards, administering public exams such as GCSEs, GCE A-levels, together with other academic and vocational qualifications, including those at entry level in the NQF. Log on to its website for more information (see *Useful contacts* for details).

» **Oxford Cambridge and RSA Examinations (OCR)**

The types of vocational qualifications provided by OCR are Skills for Life, General National Vocational Qualifications (GNVQs), NVQs, Vocational Certificates of Education (VCEs), A-levels and AS-levels, vocational GCSEs and vocational qualifications. More information can be obtained on its website (see *Useful contacts* for details).

» **City & Guilds**

City & Guilds offer a range of different qualifications, including NVQs (or SVQs in Scotland), apprenticeships and Key Skills, as well as their own qualifications. These include the following:

» *Higher Level Qualifications (HLQs):* These are designed to help you progress into a management role. They can also help you gain access into numerous higher education programmes. They offer both vocational expertise and an academic focus which can help you to climb the career ladder. The suite of HLQs comprises Higher Professional Diplomas (level 4) and Master Professional Diplomas (level 7).

» *Personal and Professional Development Awards:* These are at levels 2 and 3 (personal) and level 4 (professional). They recognise knowledge, skills and learning which are gained outside (or alongside) a formal programme of study, through work experience or a wide range of other structured activities.

» *Senior Awards:* These enable you to recognise your personal achievement and apply your professional knowledge in the workplace. They include the City & Guilds Licentiateship (LCGI), which is at supervisory or junior management level and is mapped to level 4 on the NQF; the Graduateship (GCGI), which is at middle management level and is mapped to the level of a bachelor's honours degree (level 6 on the NQF); and the Membership (MCGI), which is at a strategic management or chartered professional level and is mapped to a master's degree (level 7 of the NQF). Finally, there is the Fellowship (FCGI), which is the highest level of professional achievement.

For further information on specific qualifications, please refer to the City & Guilds website (see *Useful contacts* for details).

» LCCI Examinations Board (LCCIEB)

This provides business-related qualifications which are generally occupationally specific. LCCIEB awards have been matched to NQF levels and are available from levels 1 to 5. The qualifications issued are generally certificates or diplomas, although the Board offers a large number of NVQs. LCCIEB qualifications fall under nine general categories – business English, English language skills assessment tests, finance, general business information, technology, international languages, marketing, secretarial and business administration, and vocational access certificates. For further information regarding LCCIEB awards, consult its website (see *Useful contacts* for details).

» Welsh Joint Education Committee (WJEC)

This is an examining board primarily offering GCE A- and AS-levels and GCSEs. WJEC collaborates with AQA and City & Guilds (with which joint co-operative arrangements exist) to provide vocational qualifications in a wide variety of subject areas. The examinations are available to centres in Wales, England and Northern Ireland, although the majority are taken within Wales. Other qualifications awarded by WJEC include the level 3 Diploma in Foundation Studies (Art and Design) and Counselling Awards.

AQA, Edexcel and OCR are often referred to as the Unitary Awarding Bodies as they offer GCSE, GCE A-level, VCE A-level and GNVQ examinations. WJEC has also been collaborating with the Unitary Awarding Bodies and the Department for Education Lifelong Learning and Skills (DELLS) to ensure that VCE and GNVQ examinations are also available in the Welsh language.

Chapter 4

The qualifications

This section is a guide to what is available, starting with the entry level in the National Qualifications Framework (NQF) (and the Scottish equivalent, the Scottish Credit and Qualifications Framework (SCQF)), then moving on upward through the levels. For more information on the frameworks, see Chapter 3.

Entry level qualifications

If you want to gain a nationally recognised qualification, but you do not feel ready for GCSEs or equivalent qualifications, an entry level certificate may be for you. These qualifications are available in a wide range of subjects.

Entry level qualifications can help you build skills, increase your knowledge and boost your confidence. They are known as 'certificates' or 'awards', and are open to anyone. There are no entry requirements.

They may also be appropriate for you if you do not have traditional qualifications, or if you have been away from learning for a long time. You can also choose to take one to explore a subject that interests you.

There are over 100 entry level certificates to choose from. These include:

» traditional subjects, such as English, Science and Maths;

» skills areas, such as literacy, numeracy and life skills;

» general vocational subjects that give you a broad introduction to the world of work;

»   specific vocational subjects that tell you about a particular area of work, such as retail, hairdressing or office practice.

You can search online for entry level courses near you on the government website www.direct.gov.uk.

You can study entry level certificates at a pace that suits you as there is no set time regarding when you can take them. If you opt for certificates in National Curriculum subjects at school, they usually take one or two years to complete.

Entry level qualifications are available in a number of learning settings. They are often studied in further education colleges or school, but they can also be available in:

»   the workplace;

»   community settings through voluntary work;

»   prisons and young offenders' institutions;

»   residential or daycare settings.

Entry level qualifications are made up of a number of units, each assessed separately. This means that your achievements are recognised at every step, as you complete each unit. You are assessed on a combination of tests, assignments and tasks. These can be written, oral or practical. Often, you will also produce a portfolio that shows evidence of what you have achieved. It can contain things such as witness statements (a written or oral account of your performance), video, audio and photographs. This portfolio is assessed by teachers in your school or learning centre. You can choose to retake individual units at any time.

Different subjects and courses will vary in structure, content and the number of units. When you complete all the units, you get the full certificate.

You can take entry level qualifications at three different levels: entry 1, entry 2 and entry 3. These levels are broadly the same as the National Curriculum levels 1, 2 and 3.

'Entry level' is the first level on the NQF. The framework shows how different types of qualifications compare, in terms of the demands they place on learners.

You can progress from one entry level to the next. At entry 3, the qualifications are designed to help you move on to related qualifications at level 1 of the NQF, such as GCSEs, Key Skills, Skills for Life, National Vocational Qualifications (NVQs), BTEC Introductory (or level 1 BTEC Awards), Certificates or Diplomas or, over time, higher level qualifications. They can also lead you to work-based learning (such as an apprenticeship) or straight into a job.

Skills for Life – improving your reading, numeracy and IT skills

Do you feel held back by your lack of reading, writing, numeracy or information and communication technology skills? Or do you want to show the skills you already have in this area? There are an estimated 17.8 million people in the UK with literacy and numeracy skills below level 2, equivalent to an A* to C grade at GCSE. If you do take time to improve your skills in this area, the gain to you could be enormous.

Until not long ago 'Skills for Life' was referred to as 'Basic Skills'. The two terms mean the same thing and they refer to the same types of qualifications.

Skills for Life qualifications are designed to help you develop the skills you use in everyday life, such as reading, writing or Maths. They can also help you boost your CV or move on to further study.

You can take a Skills for Life qualification if you:

» are over 16 years of age (but in some cases, schools can also offer Skills for Life qualifications for 14 to 16 year-olds);

» have left compulsory full-time education;

» do not have an up-to-date English or Maths qualification at level 2 on the NQF (such as a GCSE).

Skills for Life Certificates are available in adult literacy, adult numeracy, and information and communication technology (ICT). There is also a Skills for Life qualification in English for Speakers of Other Languages (ESOL). The qualifications are offered on a regular basis, so you can take one whenever you are ready. They are available free of charge. You can take them in your own learning centre, a local test centre, or in some cases at a driving test centre.

Skills for Life Certificates are available at a level of learning to suit you. The levels are entry level (three entry levels to choose from), level 1 or level 2. The Skills for Life Certificate in ICT is available at entry level only. The different levels refer to the NQF (see Chapter 3). The framework shows how different types of qualifications compare, in terms of the demands they place on learners.

The type of test or task you take, and how it is assessed, will depend on which level of qualification you choose. At the three entry levels, Skills for Life qualifications consist of tasks assessed by your learning centre, college or school. At levels 1 and 2, when you are ready you will take one of the National Tests for Adult Literacy and Numeracy. Taking these will give you a clear idea of what you have achieved and what more you need to do. You can take the test on paper or on screen using a computer. The tests consist of 40 multiple choice questions. For each question, you choose from four possible answers. You have one hour to complete the literacy test and 75 minutes for the numeracy test. These are the same tests that are taken for level 1 and level 2 Key Skills qualifications in Application of Number and Communications (using Maths and writing for everyday life). If you do not pass, you can take the test again. In fact, you can take it as many times as you like until you do pass. However, each time you take it you will be asked a different set of questions.

Skills for Life qualifications are based on national standards, so everyone, including potential employers, can see what you are capable of. They can:

» give you more confidence in your own abilities;

» show what you have achieved in your learning programme;

» boost your CV;

» help you get onto other courses, such as NVQs.

To find out more, try the following sources.

» Your local further education college.

» The government website www.direct.gov.uk.

» The Qualifications and Curriculum Authority (QCA) (see *Useful contacts* for details).

» Move On Up. This is part of a campaign to encourage people to improve their literacy and numeracy skills by taking a Skills For Life qualification (see *Useful contacts* for details). You can test your basic literacy and numeracy skills on its website.

» Get On At Work. This is part of the same campaign, but it focuses on employees improving their literacy and numeracy skills to level 2 (GCSE A*–C) and gaining a national qualification. Look on the same website as above or phone 0800 100 900 for more information (lines are open from 8am to 10pm, seven days a week).

» The Basic Skills Agency (BSA) has merged with the National Institute of Adult Continuing Education (NIACE). This new organisation is the leading expert in literacy, language and numeracy across all age ranges. See www.basic-skills.co.uk.

English for Speakers of Other Languages (ESOL)

If English is not your first language, you may want to do an ESOL (English for Speakers of other Languages) course to improve your English to help you with future training and job hunting, and generally for you to get more out of your life in the UK.

ESOL courses cover speaking and listening, reading and writing, vocabulary, punctuation and grammar. There are courses at different levels so you will be able to start at the right level for you.

It is also possible to learn English online with BBC Learning English, which includes news, webcasts, quizzes and message boards for learners of English across the world, and you can also practise your skills online on the British Council's Learn English website at www. learnenglish.org.uk.

Help and advice

There are ESOL courses throughout the UK and advice is available to help you choose the right course for you. Contact Learn Direct or www.direct.gov.uk, or for free advice call the Get On helpline (tel. 0800 100 900). If you would like advice on learning and careers, you can speak to a Learn Direct adviser in the following languages:

» Farsi – 0800 093 1116

» French – 0800 093 1115

» Gujarati – 0800 093 1119

» Polish – 0800 093 1114

» Punjabi – 0800 093 1333

» Somali – 0800 093 1555

» Sylheti – 0800 093 1444

» Urdu – 0800 093 1118

» Welsh – 0800 100 900

'Life in the UK'

You must take the 'Life in the UK' test if you are applying to be a British citizen and your level of English is ESOL Entry 3 or above. If your level of English is lower than ESOL Entry 3 and you wish to apply for naturalisation, you will need to attend combined English language and citizenship classes instead. For advice on how to assess your level of English, you can contact Learn Direct or phone the Life in the UK helpline (tel. 0800 015 4245). There is also a Life in the UK website at www.lifeintheuktest.gov.uk.

Working towards a qualification with Learn Direct

Learn Direct is a government agency which provides a range of online courses to study from home, the workplace or from centres all over the country. Its courses are not qualifications as such, but many have been designed as part of learning programmes that cover the syllabuses of popular qualifications. In this way a series of Learn Direct courses can prepare and help you to work towards a qualification if you so wish.

The courses fall into the following categories:

» **Home and office IT**

There is a range of courses that develops your skills in using computers and basic IT software packages. If you are taking your very first steps in IT, then New CLAIT (Computer Literacy And Information Technology) could be for you. It will help you build your confidence and give you recognition of your skills in using computers and basic IT software packages. To get the qualification, you will need to complete a short assessment for each unit at an approved OCR CLAIT centre, such as your local college or a Learn Direct centre. This will involve completing a practical task using the appropriate software package program.

» **Specialist IT**

This range of courses covers development with specific software languages and packages, hardware and network technologies. They are geared to developing your skills for your current IT role at work, or to enable you to get your first job in IT. The relevant qualifications are the CLAIT Plus certificates and the Microsoft Office Specialist (MOS) certificates. CLAIT Plus is the next step up from New CLAIT, and Microsoft Office Specialist (MOS) is the certification scheme developed by Microsoft to recognise skills in using its Office software packages. To get the CLAIT Plus and MOS qualification you will need to pass at least three online MOS certification tests, as well as a practical task for the CLAIT Plus unit at an approved OCR/MOS assessment centre.

» ### The European Computer Driving Licence (ECDL®)

The European Computer Driving Licence Foundation is the global governing body of the world's leading computer skills certification programme, the ECDL®. This is known as the International Computer Driving Licence (ICDL®) outside Europe. The ECDL is the first qualification in personal computing skills to be recognised throughout the European Union. You might do an ECDL if you want a basic qualification in computing to enhance your career prospects, to improve your skills or just for general interest. The qualification is open to anyone, regardless of age, education, IT experience or background.

You get a logbook listing all the modules. As you pass each module, the accredited testing body will sign your logbook. You can take the modules in any order or even all at once. Normally, all tests should be completed within three years of starting. Test centres are all over Europe. You can search for one on the Learn Direct website or the ECDL Foundation's website (see *Useful contacts* for details). Centres may offer ECDL as a taught course, a flexible course or a distance learning course.

You can find details of the syllabus, sample test papers, test centres and frequently asked questions on the ECDL website. The British Computer Society is responsible for the development of the ECDL in the UK. If you are confident that you are already competent in all the skills needed for the ECDL, you will not need to undertake any training and you can just sit the test at an approved centre.

» ### Business and management

Each course looks at a specific business issue, and it includes presentation skills and personal development. Qualifications you can study for include Institute of Leadership and Management (ILM) level 2, Introductory Certificate in Team Leading ILM (Institute of Leadership & Management),

Certificate in First Line Management ILM, and the Introductory Certificate in First Line Management.

» **Languages**

Courses in a wide range of languages are offered, for beginners or those looking to brush up their existing language skills.

Key Skills qualifications

If you want to acquire or develop the skills to help you get on at school, college, work or home (or show what you already know), a Key Skills qualification could be for you. 'Key Skills' refer to the skills that are commonly needed in a range of activities in education and training, work, and life in general. They are transferable skills – once you have got them, you can use them in different situations.

Key Skills qualifications can:

» give you more confidence in your own abilities;

» boost your CV and show employers what you can do;

» help you move on to other qualifications, such as a Higher National Diploma (HND) or a degree;

» show what you have achieved in your learning programme.

These qualifications can be taken by anyone, from school students to chief executives of large companies. There are no minimum entry requirements, and you can study them alongside other types of qualifications, such as GCSEs.

You can take Key Skills qualifications in any approved centre, from schools and colleges to training providers. They are also offered by some employers, the armed forces and the Prison Service. You can study Key Skills as part of a full-time or part-time course at school or college (such as an NVQ or as part of an apprenticeship – see Chapter 5), or as part of some higher education courses.

There are six different Key Skills subjects: Main Key Skills in Communication, Application of Number (numeracy skills), ICT (information and communication technology), Wider Key Skills in Working with Others, Improving Own Learning and Performance and Problem Solving. Key Skills are at levels 1 to 4 of the NQF. You can take different subjects at different levels to suit you.

HOW YOU ARE ASSESSED

Each Key Skill is assessed separately. Your assessment is based on a portfolio you produce, which is assessed internally by your school, college or trainer. This will be a folder of evidence that shows that you have the necessary skills to pass. For the three main Key Skills, you also take a test, which is marked externally by an awarding body. At levels 1 and 2, the test consists of 40 multiple choice questions, each with four possible answers. The test lasts for an hour, or 75 minutes for Application of Number at level 3. It lasts for 90 minutes and you have to write your answers to the questions, or complete a practical task for the ICT test. The test at level 4 lasts for two and a half hours. You can take a practice test online for the three main Key Skills qualifications at the 'keyskills4u' website at www.keyskills4u.com.

WHERE THEY CAN LEAD

Getting a Key Skills qualification at one level can lead to further Key Skills qualifications at higher levels. They can also help you move on to other qualifications, such as an HND or bachelor's degree.

HELP AND ADVICE

Speak to your teacher at school or college, visit the 'keyskills4u' website or ask your employer about Key Skills courses available where you work. You can also consult Connexions or Learn Direct.

The Learning and Skills Development Agency (LSDA) has a Key Skills Support Programme helpline (for schools and colleges) and you can contact the agency on 0870 872 8081. For enquiries about work-based Key Skills, contact the Learning for Work helpline on 0845 602 3386 or email helpline@lfw.org.uk.

You can phone the QCA enquiry line on 020 7509 5555 or take a look at its website (see *Useful contacts* for details). You can also look at the Department for Children, Schools and Families' Key Skills website at www.dfes.gov.uk or the Key Skills Support Programme site at www.keyskillssupport.net.

General Certificate of Secondary Education (GCSE)

GCSEs are the main qualification taken by 14 to 16 year-olds, but they are available to anyone who would like to study a subject that interests them. You can take GCSEs in a wide range of academic and 'applied' (work-related) subjects. They are highly valued by schools, colleges and employers, so they will be useful whatever you are planning to do afterwards.

The qualification mainly involves studying the theory of a subject, combined with some investigative work. Some subjects also involve practical work. GCSEs are usually studied full time at school or college, and they take five terms to complete. GCSEs are at levels 1 and 2 on the NQF, depending on the grade you get. To achieve high grades, you will usually be expected to show good levels of attainment in reading and writing.

» Grades D to G are at level 1.

» Grades A* to C are at level 2.

GCSEs are available in more than 40 academic and eight vocational subjects. See more about vocational GCSEs on page 79. If you are a student in Years 10 and 11 (aged 14 to 16), it's compulsory to study some subjects as part of the National Curriculum.

If you have left school with poor GCSE results, do not be put off. There may be a lot of reasons why you did not do well. Perhaps school did not bring out the best in you, or perhaps you had little interest in the subjects being studied, or perhaps you feel that you are more mature now. You can study for more GCSEs at any time in your life.

HOW YOU ARE ASSESSED

With GCSEs, you are assessed mainly on written exams, plus elements of coursework that you complete throughout the course. Coursework can include projects, fieldwork, artwork, experiments or investigations. Some subjects, like art and design, have more coursework and fewer exams.

Some GCSE courses are made up of short courses, or units. For these, you take exams at the end of each unit. Other GCSEs involve exams at the end of the course. For some subjects, everyone sits the same exam. For other subjects, you have a choice of two tiers: 'higher' or 'foundation'. Each tier leads to a different range of grades. Higher tier exams lead to grades A* to D and foundation tier exams lead to grades C to G. Your subject teacher normally decides which tier is best for you.

WHERE THEY CAN LEAD

Getting a GCSE can lead to a number of routes; for example, work, further study or an apprenticeship. If you complete GCSEs at level 1, you could move on to other courses or work-based training at levels 1 or 2. Completing GCSEs at level 2 can lead to other level 2 courses and level 3 courses of all types. However, sometimes if you want to take a level 3 course (such as an A-level), you will be expected to have a GCSE in the same subject. If you are thinking about higher education, you may need GCSEs in certain subjects. Most universities and colleges will ask for five GCSEs grades (A* to C), including English and Maths (as well as A-levels or equivalent qualifications).

HELP AND ADVICE

For more information, contact Connexions if you are 19 or under, or if you are over 19, Learn Direct. If you are at school, talk to your subject and career teachers to help you decide what plan of action will be best for you after Year 11. *It's Your Choice* is a useful guide, if you are a Year 10 or Year 11 student, to help plan your next steps after Year 11. Visit www.connexions-direct.com/its yourchoice. Jobs4U is the Connexions occupational database that helps you find out different entry levels for jobs and you can find out whether you need to undertake full-time learning after Year 11. Visit www.connexions-direct.com/jobs4u.

You can search for GCSE courses near you on www.direct. gov.uk, or contact your local college. The Learn Direct courses database lets you search for hundreds of courses throughout the country. Visit www.learndirect-advice.co.uk/findacourse. UK250 provides links to many colleges and its official website gives lots of useful information (see www.uk250.co.uk/College). You can, of course, also ask to receive any college prospectus by post. Most colleges hold an open day which will give you the opportunity to find out more about the institution, to talk to subject tutors and to ask any questions. It is worth asking the college if it can offer you a more flexible way of learning. For example, if you have a disability, you may be able to work from home and receive extra practical help when you are taking your exams.

You can also contact the awarding bodies for GCSEs for more information on the subjects you can study, and any particular entry requirements (see Chapter 3).

Vocational GCSEs

Vocational GCSEs (also referred to as 'applied GCSEs') exist to introduce students to a broad sector of industry or business, to improve job or apprenticeship prospects. They are designed to offer a more practical hands-on approach to learning, being both academic and vocational. You can choose from a range of applied subjects, including applied art and design, applied business, applied ICT, applied science, engineering, health and social care, leisure and tourism, manufacturing, hospitality and catering, construction and the built environment, applied physical education and applied French.

These GCSEs are available to 14 to 16 year-olds at school, but it is possible to study for them if you are over 16.

They are assessed at the same standard as traditional GCSEs, although the work you produce will have a more practical emphasis. You will carry out your own investigations and produce a portfolio of work. The qualification is made up of three units of equal value. Normally, two-thirds of your work is assessed by your teachers, and one-third by external examiners. If you are at school, your lessons for taking a vocational GCSE may take place in a local college.

Because many applied GCSEs are double the size of traditional GCSEs, they are graded A*A* to GG and U (unclassified). Grades DD to GG are at level 1 and grades A*A* to CC are at level 2.

BTECs and OCR Nationals

BTEC qualifications and OCR Nationals are particular types of work-related qualifications, available in a wide range of subjects. If you find studying boring or difficult, and you do not think that you will do well at exams, these courses may be for you. They are recognised qualifications based on relevant work experience. You can take one if you are interested in learning more about a particular sector or industry, but it does not mean that you cannot change your mind about what you want to do, as many of the skills you learn will serve you well in any job.

Many have been designed in collaboration with industry, so they can equip you with the skills and knowledge that employers are looking for. The qualifications offer a mix of theory and practice, and they can also include an element of work experience. They can take the form of (or be part of) a technical certificate – one of the key components of an apprenticeship (see Chapter 5).

They are available in a wide range of subjects, including:

» Art and design

» Leisure and tourism

» Business

» IT

» Health and social care

» Early years (the care and education of children from birth to the age of eight)

» Media

» Public services

» Science

» Sport

The qualifications are usually studied full time at college, or sometimes at school (or in collaboration between a school and college). You can also take them part time at college. They are mainly taken by learners over 16 including adults, although some schools offer them to 14 to 16 year-olds, normally in combination with other qualifications, such as GCSEs or Key Skills.

BTEC qualifications are available at various levels on the NQF, and some short courses are outside the NQF. OCR Nationals are offered at levels 1 to 3. Within each level, the qualifications are available in a range of sizes, taking different amounts of time to complete. By their nature BTEC short courses concentrate on relatively small blocks of learning within a specific focused area of activity, employment sector or skills area. Here are the main BTEC qualifications:

» **BTEC Introductory Certificate and Diplomas**

These are designed to widen participation and improve performance at level 1 of the NQF. They encourage you to develop the personal skills and attributes needed for you to improve your confidence in your ability to work, learn and achieve your full potential.

» **BTEC First Certificate and Diplomas**

These are NQF level 2 vocational qualifications which provide the initial knowledge and understanding you need before you choose a job in a particular area or move on to further study at level 3. They can be taken in subjects such as agriculture, animal care, IT applications, motor vehicle studies, performing arts and public services. The First Diploma is a full-time course studied over a year. The courses encourage the development of personal and work-related skills, and provide a foundation for work or a progression on to further study. The course is divided into six units in the subject area, all of which you will need to complete.

» **BTEC National Award, National Certificate and National Diplomas**

These programmes are related to broad occupational areas such as engineering, fashion, music, photography, sports science and public services. They are designed to train specialists or technician-level workers. Each qualification is equivalent in terms of standard, but differs in terms of the number of units required for successful completion. To achieve the National Award, you will need six BTEC qualifications; to achieve the National Certificate, you will need 12 BTEC qualifications; and for the National Diploma, 18. The National Award is comparable in standard and breadth to one GCE A-level; the BTEC National Certificate to two GCE A-levels and the BTEC National Diploma to three GCE A-levels.

More advanced BTEC specialist awards are also available to train higher technicians and para-professionals. These are Higher National Certificate and Diploma (HNC/HND) qualifications, and foundation degrees, which are discussed later on in this chapter.

ENTRY REQUIREMENTS

Qualifications at different levels can have different entry requirements. For example, if you want to study for a level 2 qualification, you will generally need GCSEs grades D to G, or a level 1 qualification in a similar subject. To study a level 3 qualification, you will normally need GCSEs grades A* to C, or a level 2 qualification in a related subject.

HOW YOU ARE ASSESSED

Generally, you are assessed by your teacher or trainer in your place of study. Depending on the qualification you choose, some assessment may also be done by external examiners.

Rather than written exam papers, you will complete a range of assignments, case studies and practical activities, as well as a portfolio of evidence that shows the work you have completed. BTEC and OCR Nationals are graded pass, merit or distinction. You can also get a certificate for a single unit, so you gain recognition as you progress.

WHERE THEY CAN LEAD

BTECs or OCR Nationals can lead to a job or further study. For example, you could progress from a qualification at one level on the NQF to higher levels in the same or related area of study. This could eventually lead to professional qualifications. You could also use a level 3 qualification as a route into higher education, such as taking an HNC or HND.

HELP AND ADVICE

BTEC qualifications are offered by the awarding body Edexcel and OCR Nationals by the awarding body Oxford Cambridge and RSA Examinations (see *Useful contacts* for details). Visit their websites to find out about the specific qualifications on offer. You can also get advice from your school or college, Connexions or Learn Direct, but your employer may also have information as well, as many of these qualifications are work related.

General Certificate of Education AS and A-levels

If you want to study a particular subject in detail, AS- (Advanced Subsidiary) and A- (Advanced) level qualifications may be for you. Most employers are familiar with them and they are usually highly rated, especially by employers. Qualifications focus on traditional study skills. They normally take two years to complete full time in school or college, although they are also available to study part time. You can choose from a wide range of academic subjects, as well as some 'applied' (work-related) subjects. AS- and A-levels are at level 3 on the NQF.

A-levels are made up of the AS-level and the A2. Each part makes up 50 per cent of the overall A-level grade. The AS-level can be either a free-standing qualification, or be valued as the first half of the full A-level. At the end of the AS year, you can choose to either take the AS-level only, or continue to the second year and go for the full A-level.

In year two of a full A-level, you take the A2 – this is not a separate qualification, but rather the second half of the A-level. The A2 is designed to deepen the knowledge you gained during the AS-level. If you are expecting to get an A grade at A-level, you may also want to consider taking an Advanced Extension Award (AEA) (see page 86).

From September 2008, there will only be four papers for most A-level papers. At present there are six.

There are about 80 AS- and A-level subjects available. Most school and college students take three or four AS-levels in the first year of an A-level. This means that you can keep your options open about which subjects to study as a full A-level.

Vocational Certificates of Education (VCEs)

Vocational Certificates of Education (VCEs) (also known as vocational, or applied, A-levels) have been introduced to improve the standing of vocational qualifications and to increase flexibility within the system. As far as university entry is concerned, VCE A-levels have the same status as conventional GCE A-levels.

Aimed at developing skills and understanding as well as specific knowledge, VCEs are appropriate for subjects such as art and design, catering or engineering. Every subject covers skills in communication, numeracy, IT, problem solving and working as a team, while work placements help put your learning into practice. The emphasis is on coursework rather than examination grades, so think carefully about which you prefer before making your choices.

Applied A-levels consist of six units and they normally take two years to complete, but, like A-levels, you can take a three-unit AS-level over one year. If you want to take the subject further, you can take a 12-unit Applied A-level Double Award, which is equivalent to two A-levels. This comprises six compulsory and six optional units. The VCEs may be studied in conjunction with general A- or AS-levels.

ENTRY REQUIREMENTS

You can take AS- and A-level qualifications whether you are a school student (Years 12 and 13) or an adult. In most cases, you need at least five GCSEs at grades A* to C. Sometimes, you need a grade B or above at GCSE in a particular subject to take it at AS- or A-level. Some schools and colleges also ask that you have GCSE grade C or above in English and Maths.

HOW YOU ARE ASSESSED

The AS-level and A2 are each made up of three units. You are normally assessed on a mixture of 70 per cent written exams and 30 per cent coursework. There is an assessment of practical skills in some subjects, such as Science or Art. All A-levels must also include some 'synoptic assessment' as part of the A2. This means that it will test your understanding of the whole subject, and it will normally contribute to 20 per cent to the full A-level. AS- and A-levels are graded A to E. Your results slip will also show a score on something called the 'uniform mark scale' (UMS). The AS-level is scored out of 300 UMS marks, and the A-level out of 600 marks.

WHERE THEY CAN LEAD

A- and AS-levels are one of the main routes into employment or higher education. Different qualifications have been allocated points in what is called the UCAS Tariff (a system operated by the Universities and Colleges Admissions Service (UCAS)). The points for the qualifications you have will be totalled to see if they meet the minimum required for the higher education course, or the college or university. For example, one A-level with an A grade has 120 UCAS points. If you have grades C, D and E at GCE A-level, this will amount to 180 points on the UCAS Tariff.

Advanced Extension Awards (AEAs)

Advanced Extension Awards (AEAs) ask you to use the knowledge you have gained during your A-level studies and then apply it more widely and critically than in the A-level exam. Because they are designed for the top ten per cent of students, they also allow universities to tell the difference between the most able candidates, especially in subjects where many students get A grades. The AEA is at level 3 on the NQF.

AEAs are normally taken by students studying A-levels, so there is no need to attend extra classes or learn new topics. However, it is possible to take the AEA without the A-level itself. They are available in 19 subjects. In most cases, it is advisable for you to be studying (or to have finished studying) an A-level in the same subject.

HOW YOU ARE ASSESSED

You take a written exam that is assessed by external examiners. You will be expected to demonstrate your use of critical analysis, good evaluation skills and the ability to pull together different topics. There are two pass grades for an AEA, which are distinction and merit.

WHERE THEY CAN LEAD

Many people who take an AEA will go on to higher education; for example, studying for a degree. Areas count towards the UCAS Tariff if you want to get into higher education. A distinction is worth 40 points, and a merit 20. This is over and above the points you get for your A-levels.

However, even if you are not planning to go on to higher education, the qualification is worth taking as it may make all the difference in helping you to get the job you want.

HELP AND ADVICE

You can find out more about these qualifications, including how to apply, from the school or college offering the course. You can also get advice from Connexions or Learn Direct.

Access courses

Access courses are aimed at adults (the minimum age is 19) who want to study but do not have the necessary qualifications to get into higher education. They are an ideal way to get you back into studying by introducing you to not only the subject, but how you can learn at this level. Access courses are usually run at local colleges, and take up to a year to complete. However, they are flexible and some people take their time and study over two years.

You will usually have a choice as to whether to study full or part time. You will be introduced to the study skills you need, such as taking notes and revising, writing essays or reports and researching topics in the library or on the internet. Access courses start off with a gentle introduction to study, but by the end you will have all the knowledge and skills you need to progress to higher education and achieve the qualifications you are aiming for. You will have also spent a year or more studying alongside people who have goals and aspirations like yourself, which can be a great source of support.

Courses usually cover a broad subject area; for example, business, science or humanities (which touches on geography, history and other subjects). This means that you can begin to study even if you are not yet sure what course or qualification you eventually want to aim for. Your tutors on the course will be able to help you make the right choice and will help with any application to higher education that you decide to make.

International Baccalaureate (IB)

The International Baccalaureate (IB) Diploma can be taken as an alternative to GCE A-levels. Unlike A-levels, the International Baccalaureate (IB) Diploma Programme is more wide ranging, covering a variety of different subject areas, rather than just the one.

The IB Diploma Programme is recognised in over 100 countries and it is becoming a more popular choice among UK students, as well as those who have only recently taken up residence to the country. At the time of writing it is only available at 87 schools and colleges in the UK, but the government has announced that it will be available across the country by 2010. Leading to a single qualification, rather than separate qualifications for individual subjects, the programme can be taken in English, French or Spanish.

It is designed to encourage you to learn how to learn, ask challenging questions, develop a strong sense of your own identity and culture, and develop the ability to communicate with and understand people from other countries and cultures. The IB Diploma Programme is at level 3 on the NQF, and is made up of a compulsory 'core', plus six separate subjects where you have some choice over what you study. Normally, you will study three of your six optional subjects at a 'higher' level (240 teaching hours per subject), and the other three at a 'standard' level (150 teaching hours). However, you can also opt to take four subjects at the higher level and two at the standard level.

HOW YOU ARE ASSESSED

Most of the assessment is carried out through exams, marked externally. However, in nearly all subjects, some of the assessment is carried out by your teachers, who mark individual pieces of coursework. The diploma normally takes two years to complete, with exams taking place in May and November. You are awarded points for each part of the programme, up to a maximum of 45 – up to seven points for each of the six optional subjects you take and up to three points from your performance in the core elements. To achieve a full diploma, you must score 24 points or more. However, if you do not achieve the full diploma, you will be awarded a certificate for each subject taken.

WHERE THEY CAN LEAD

The IB is considered to offer a broader, more enriching qualification by many teachers and higher education institutions.

Most students who take the IB Diploma Programme go on to higher education. The qualification is recognised by universities in more than 100 countries. However, you may be asked to gain a certain number of points at the 'higher' level in specific subjects if you want to study a particular course.

From 2008 entry onwards, successfully completing the diploma will officially count towards your UCAS Tariff for getting into higher education in the UK. An IB Diploma total of 24 points will earn 280 UCAS points – the same as two Bs and a C grade at A-level. The maximum of 45 points will earn 768 UCAS points – equivalent to more than six A-levels at grade A.

HELP AND ADVICE

You can get more information about the IB Diploma Programme, including a list of schools and colleges that offer it, from the International Baccalaureate Organisation. The Connexions service will also advise you.

Note that the Welsh Baccalaureate Qualification, also known as WBQ or Welsh Bac, is a pre-university qualification which may be offered in the future to schools and colleges in Wales. If it is offered, the WBQ would replace A-levels and possibly many other courses and tests. 31 schools and colleges have been running a pilot scheme since 2005. The Welsh Assembly Government intends that one-quarter of Welsh students will be studying for the qualification by 2010.

Higher National Certificates and Higher National Diplomas

If you want to extend your education and gain a recognised qualification to do a specific job, a BTEC HNC or a HND could be for you. HNCs and HNDs are vocational higher education qualifications which focus on 'learning by doing'. They can lead straight to a career, or they can help you progress in your current career.

They are highly valued by employers both in the UK and overseas and they can also count towards membership by professional bodies and other employer organisations. HNCs and HNDs are provided by over 400 higher education colleges and further education colleges.

HNCs can take one year to complete full time. However, you can study for this qualification part time at college or by distance learning, usually for two years. An HNC is often studied part time by students who are also in a job. They are at level 4 on the NQF (see Chapter 3).

HNDs take two years full time and they can also be taken part time for a longer period. They are at level 5 on the NQF. They comprise core units (which are compulsory) and specialist units (which are optional and designed to provide flexibility with the exact focus of the qualification). The number of units required for successful completion of the new awards is ten for the HNC and 16 for the HND. Each unit should take approximately 60 hours to study.

The qualifications are available in a wide range of subject areas, including:

» Agriculture

» Accounting

» Business and management

» Computing and IT

» Construction and civil engineering

» Engineering

» Health and social care

» Hospitality management

» Performing arts

» Retail and distribution

» Sport and exercise sciences

To study for an HNC or HND, you will need some previous qualifications. Most HND courses require one A-level (or equivalent). The qualifications are offered mostly at higher education colleges and some universities.

HOW YOU ARE ASSESSED

The qualifications are mainly assessed through assignments, projects and practical tasks that you complete throughout the course. If you successfully complete an HNC or HND, the grades in each subject unit are shown as pass, merit or distinction.

WHERE THEY CAN LEAD

Because HNCs and HNDs are designed to give you the skills for a particular field of work, they can lead straight to a career. You can also use the qualifications to progress within your current career; for example, as a stepping stone to gaining professional status. If you complete an HNC, you may wish to choose to go into higher education. You can also convert your HNC or HND to a bachelor's degree with extra study. Once you complete your course, HNCs can allow entry into the second year of a degree, while HNDs can allow entry into the second or third year.

BTEC Higher Nationals form much of the basis upon which new foundation degrees have been developed (see page 90).

HELP AND ADVICE

BTEC qualifications are offered by the Edexcel awarding body. Visit its website (see *Useful contacts*) to find out about the specific qualifications on offer. You can also get advice from your school or college, Connexions or Learn Direct, but your employer may also have information as the qualifications are work related. You can look for HNC or HND courses near you on the government's website at www.direct.gov.uk, including details of the specific entry requirements for a particular course. You can also search for courses on the UCAS website (see *Useful contacts* for details).

Certificates and Diplomas of Higher Education

Both the Certificate of Higher Education (CertHE) and the Diploma of Higher Education (DipHE) are accredited professional qualifications highly respected by employers both in the UK and overseas.

Certificates of Higher Education are academic, rather than vocational qualifications. They are broadly the academic equivalent to an HNC, and usually take a year of full-time study to complete. They are at 'certificate' level on the Framework for Higher Education Qualifications (FHEQ). In Scotland, a CertHE is worth 120 credit points at level 7 on the SCQF (see Chapter 3 for more information). (As a guide, an Honours degree is worth 480 credit points.)

Diplomas of Higher Education are similar to HNDs. They usually take two years to complete and offer subjects such as accounting, construction, engineering, nursing, science, technology and textile design. The diplomas are at 'intermediate' level on the FHEQ. In Scotland a DipHE is worth 240 credit points (at least 120 at level 7 and at least 80 at level 8) on the SCQF. (As a guide, an Honours degree is worth 360 credit points.)

ENTRY REQUIREMENTS

There are no set entry requirements. Check with the university or college to see if you have the necessary experience or qualifications to do a particular CertHE or DipHE.

HOW YOU ARE ASSESSED

Different courses will assess you in different ways. Most courses involve a mixture of exams and coursework. Some ask you for a written dissertation that you produce at the end of the course.

WHERE THEY CAN LEAD

CertHEs or DipHEs can often lead straight to a job, due to their professional content. You can also use your qualification to progress to a bachelor's degree with further study (this normally takes about two years if you have a CertHE and one year if you have a DipHE).

HELP AND ADVICE

You can find out more about CertHEs or DipHEs, including how to apply, from the university or college offering the course. You can also get advice from your school or college, Connexions or Learn Direct. You can also search for courses on the UCAS website (see *Useful contacts* for details).

Bachelor's degree

A bachelor's degree (sometimes known as an 'ordinary' or 'first' degree) is a course of academic study leading to a qualification such as a Bachelor of Arts (BA), Bachelor of Science (BSc) or Bachelor of Medicine (BM). Bachelor's degrees are at 'intermediate' and 'honours' level on the FHEQ (see Chapter 3).

It usually takes three or four years to complete full time (normally four years if you are doing a sandwich course, which includes a year in industry or abroad). However, bachelor's degrees in certain subjects can take longer; for example, medical courses usually take five or six years. Many degrees can be studied part time. You can study at universities, higher education colleges or via distance or flexible learning (e.g. the Open University).

The qualification is designed to give you a thorough understanding of a subject. It helps you develop your analytical and intellectual skills, and it can also broaden your horizons and make you challenge yourself. There are a vast number of different bachelor's degree courses to choose from. Some subjects, such as medicine, law and architecture, prepare you for a particular career. Others, like English or history, can equip you with skills for a wide range of jobs.

ENTRY REQUIREMENTS

To study for a bachelor's degree, you will usually need to have some previous qualifications. If you have any qualification at level 3 on the FHEQ (see Chapter 3 for more information), you can earn points on the UCAS Tariff for entry into higher education. Different courses will ask for a different number of points. Both BTEC and OCR Nationals can earn you equivalent points to AS- and A-levels. For example, a BTEC National Diploma with overall three merit grades has 240 UCAS points (one A-level with an A grade has 120 UCAS points).

Most bachelor's degrees ask for at least two A-levels at grade E or above (or equivalent grades in other qualifications). If the university is regarded as particularly high status (e.g. Oxford or Cambridge) or it is a leader in your chosen subject area, the entry qualifications will be higher grades at A-level and there may be a separate entry examination or other form of assessment. To find out the entrance requirements for a particular course, you can do a search on the UCAS website (see *Useful contacts* for details), or read the course prospectus – most are now available online.

You may be classed as a mature student if you are over 21 when you start your course. Mature students come from all backgrounds and life experiences, often having worked or brought up children, or sometimes both, in the years before they go into higher education. It is impossible to generalise about a 'typical' mature student because there is no such thing, and there is no upper age limit. If you are a mature student, higher education institutions are often flexible about entry requirements, especially if you can show your commitment to study and learning (some recent experience of study will help further). It will also help your case if you can show particular interest and some knowledge of the subject you want to study. Do not automatically assume, because you do not have formal qualifications, that you cannot apply to do a bachelor's degree. Talk to the course provider and he will be able to advise you on the best steps to take. You may find it useful to take an access course as a stepping stone to doing a bachelor's degree (see page 87).

HOW YOU ARE ASSESSED

Different courses will assess you in different ways. Bachelor's degrees may involve a mixture of exams and coursework, or they may be totally exam based or coursework based. Some ask you for a written dissertation that you produce at the end of the course. The different grades, in descending order, are first, upper second (2:1), lower second (2:2), third, pass and fail. If you get the grade third or above, you get a bachelor's degree with honours (BA Hons).

WHERE THEY CAN LEAD

Most graduates use their bachelor's degree to move into a job or profession. You can also use the qualification to go on to a postgraduate course of higher education, such as a diploma or master's degree. Studying for a degree shows employers that you are resourceful enough to commit yourself to a great deal of study. Employers look for evidence of self-awareness and interpersonal skills, such as leadership and communication. You can demonstrate and develop these through joining university clubs and societies.

HELP AND ADVICE

To find out more about bachelor's degree courses, including how to apply, see page 93. You can also get advice from your school or college, Connexions or Learn Direct. You can also search for courses on the UCAS and Open University websites (see *Useful contacts* for details). Bachelor's degree courses start throughout the year, although most begin in September or October. Check individual prospectuses to find out about starting dates for particular courses.

Family commitments and work responsibilities are often an important issue for older students. This has been recognised by the government and higher education institutions, which provide special support for students with children and special circumstances. Grants and benefits are available to parents who want to study, and tuition fees are paid for most independent students over the age of 25. For advice about financing your education, see Chapter 7.

Foundation degree

Foundation degrees are particular types of degree that are designed to equip you with the skills and knowledge that employers are looking for. It can lead straight to a job, or prepare you for developing your professional skills in the future. Studying for the qualification provides technical knowledge and understanding in the subject area, to improve your prospects if you are planning a career where you will be working closely with professionals. Foundation degrees cover a wide range of vocational subjects including veterinary nursing, legal executive, marketing, human resources, e-commerce, health and social care, forensic science, hotel management and aircraft engineering. In essence, the degrees are designed to combine academic study with workplace learning.

The qualification is at 'intermediate' level on the FHEQ. It is broadly equivalent to the first two years of a bachelor's degree.

Foundation degrees are offered by a growing number of higher education and further education colleges. You learn in a way that suits you, through distance or online learning, in the workplace or online. It takes around two years to complete a foundation degree full time, or three to four years part time. There are over 1,700 courses running, with a further 900 planned. They have been developed to be flexible and if you are working, it allows you to continue with your studies.

ENTRY REQUIREMENTS

There are no set entry requirements. Check with the university or college to see if you have the necessary experience or qualifications to do a particular foundation degree, or search for foundation degree courses at the UCAS website (see *Useful contacts* for details).

HOW YOU ARE ASSESSED

Different foundation degree courses will assess you in different ways. Most courses involve a mixture of exams and coursework, plus an assessment of the learning you do in the workplace. Some ask you for a written dissertation that you produce at the end of the course. Generally, there are no grades for foundation degrees; in most cases you are awarded either a 'pass' or 'fail'. However, a few courses may also offer a 'distinction'.

WHERE THEY CAN LEAD

Foundation degrees can often lead straight to a job, as they are designed in collaboration with businesses. You can also use your foundation degree to progress to a bachelor's degree with further study (this normally takes about a year).

HELP AND ADVICE

You can find out more about foundation degrees, including how to apply, from Foundation Degree Forward (see *Useful contacts*) and www.foundationdegree.org.uk. The Aimhigher website (see *Useful contacts* for details) provides information on foundation degrees and vocational education for anyone who is thinking of continuing or returning to their studies. You can also get advice from your school or college, Connexions or Learn Direct, but also your employer may have information as the qualifications are work related.

Postgraduate qualifications

There is a wide variety of postgraduate qualification courses on offer at universities and other higher education institutions. You may want to consider enrolling for a course to enhance your job prospects in your chosen career. Alternatively, you may want to retrain in a different area to attain the next step in your career; for example, in law, teaching or librarianship. You may want to study your degree subject in more depth, for pure enjoyment or to open up further research possibilities. Generally, there are four main types of postgraduate qualification:

» **Postgraduate certificate (PGCert) and postgraduate diploma (PGDip)**

Although the content is academic, these are primarily vocational.

» **Master's degree**

A qualification of academic study, although some master's degrees are also vocational. The types of master's degree available include:

   » MA: Master of Arts

   » MSc: Master of Science

   » MBA: Master of Business Administration

   » LLM: Master of Law

   » MEd: Master of Education

   » MPhil: Master of Philosophy

» MRes: Master of Research

» **Doctorate (PhD)**

Qualifications of academic study

Most types of postgraduate qualification will include taught and research elements, although some are entirely taught or entirely research based.

Taught courses

With these courses you work through modules and units, learning in a similar way to your first degree. Taught courses usually take nine months to a year to complete full time, although some institutions offer students the chance to study part time, spreading modules over two or three years. Some courses are work related, for students who studied other subjects at college and want to retrain; for example, in IT. Taught courses can lead to a range of qualifications, including an MA, MSc, MBA, PGDip or PGCert. They can also be the first step towards a PhD.

Taught courses are often linked to a specific profession. Here are some examples:

» **Postgraduate Certificate of Education (PGCE)**

This qualifies you as a teacher. It takes one year to complete full time, and you can get financial help from the government while you study. You can also take a PGCE part time at some universities.

» **Graduate Diploma in Legal Studies**

This is also known as the 'Common Professional Exam' and it allows you to begin training in law if you have not already studied it as part of your degree. This can be a first step towards a career in law. If you have done a three-year degree in law, the next stage is a vocational qualification called the 'Legal Practice', which lasts one year full time.

» **Information Management and Librarianship and Information Studies**

This is a postgraduate diploma if you are interested in a career as a librarian.

» **Postgraduate diploma or MSc or MA in social work**

If your first degree is not related to social work and you would like to train for this profession, you can apply to study for a diploma or higher degree in social work.

Research based

You will have the opportunity to undertake an original piece of research, with guidance from a supervisor. He will advise you on whether your research is on track and about the deadlines you have to meet.

ENTRY REQUIREMENTS

Some, but not all, postgraduate qualifications require that you already have a bachelor's degree. Some, particularly postgraduate research degrees, will expect you to have a lower second (2:2) and sometimes an upper second (2:1) or above in the same or a related subject area. To find out the entry requirements for a particular postgraduate course, you can search for courses online at the website www.direct.gov.uk and you can also contact the institution offering them.

HOW YOU ARE ASSESSED

With taught courses there may be continuous assessment and exams, and you may have to do a dissertation at the end of the course. The method of assessment will vary depending on the type of course and the institution. Grades are normally awarded as distinction, merit, pass or fail.

A master's degree can be research based, a taught course or a mixture of both, and will take at least 12 months of full-time study to complete. The amount of lectures, seminars, projects and research papers will vary depending on the type of course and the institution. You may also have to submit a dissertation at the end of your course. Most master's degrees are normally awarded as distinction, merit, pass and fail or distinction, pass and fail.

A doctorate qualification gives you the opportunity to undertake an original piece of research. It will usually take at least three years of full-time study to complete. Throughout the course, you will be expected to work independently, with guidance from a supervisor. The supervisor advises you on whether your research is on track and about deadlines you have to meet. During the first one to three years of your doctorate, you will research your chosen topic and plan your dissertation. In your final year, you will normally write up your dissertation. Many doctorate courses lead to a qualification such as a Doctor of Philosophy (a PhD or Dphil). Doctorates are usually awarded as either a pass or fail; in a few cases with a distinction.

WHERE THEY CAN LEAD

Postgraduate certificates can lead on to postgraduate diplomas. You can also use a postgraduate certificate or diploma as a route into a specific career or onto further study, such as a master's degree.

Some master's degrees, such as in business administration or law, prepare you for a career in a particular field. Others, like the Master of Research, can prepare you for a doctorate qualification.

HELP AND ADVICE

To find out more about getting a postgraduate qualification, contact the universities and colleges, or visit their websites. Their prospectuses will list both taught courses and research opportunities. Some colleges have a postgraduate open day, which is a chance for you to meet prospective tutors or supervisors. The Higher Education and Research Opportunities (HERO) website (see *Useful contacts*) also has information about research careers and funding. The Association of MBAs (see *Useful contacts*) represents universities and colleges that offer Masters of Business Administration. You can also search for postgraduate courses online at www.direct.gov.uk.

Qualifications specific to Wales

These courses taught in Wales are in addition to the ones referred to previously.

» **Modern Skills Diplomas for Adults (MSDAs)**

These are Welsh qualifications designed for people above the age of 25 with the purpose of improving the skill level of the workforce. The diploma course is a mixture of work-based training, NVQs, Key Skills and other relevant vocational qualifications. It is an NQF level 3 award and entry is usually restricted to adults with an educational level equivalent to NQF level 2 (see Chapter 3 for more information).

» **Certificate in Office Skills**

This is a basic vocational qualification for office-based workers. Its modules cover topics such as word processing, shorthand, database processing and computerised accounts.

» **Vocational Units in Welsh Second Language**

The awarding body of the Welsh Joint Education Committee (WJEC) offers vocational qualifications in Welsh as a second language. There are three levels of award in line with other NQF qualifications, which are the Foundation Award, Intermediate Award and Advanced Subsidiary Vocational Certificate of Education.

Qualifications specific to Scotland

This is a guide to courses taught in Scotland's schools and further education colleges.

National Qualifications (NQs)

NQs are designed to let you study at a level that suits you. You can take them at school, but they are available to adults at colleges and some training centres. They cover a wide range of subjects, from chemistry to construction, history to hospitality, and computing to care. National qualifications are divided into five levels: Access, Intermediate 1, Intermediate 2, Higher and Advanced Higher, but not all subjects are available at the full range of levels.

The types of NQ that you will come across are Standard Grades, National Units, National Courses and Group Awards:

Standard Grades

These are generally taken over the third and fourth year at secondary schools. Students often take seven or eight subjects, including Maths and English. There are three levels of study: Credit, General and Foundation. Students usually take exams at two levels which are Credit and General or General and Foundation.

The Standard Grade system is now being slowly phased out in favour of the Scottish Qualifications Authority (SQA) Higher Still system. Higher Still covers five levels of qualifications, which are Access, Intermediate 1, Intermediate 2, Higher and Advanced Higher.

National Units (available at SCQF levels 1 to 7)

These are approximately 40 hours in design length. National Units form the basis of National Courses and Scottish Group Awards (SGAs), but they are also frequently taken as free-standing units and are certificated as such. You can take National Units on their own at any of the seven levels. You will be awarded a pass in a Unit when you have achieved all of the unit outcomes. Individual National Units are not graded. You will receive a certificate for each one completed.

National Courses (available at SCQF levels 4 to 7)

At levels 4 to 7 you can take a National Course. This is usually made up of three National Units of 40 hours, although some are fractions (e.g. 20 hours) or multiples (e.g. 80 hours). The number of units will vary if 20- or 80-hour units are used. An additional time allocation of 40 hours is usually allowed to let you integrate learning across the course and to help you prepare for the external assessment. As a result, the timetabling recommended for each course is 160 hours. All courses are the same length, whatever the level. There is also an external assessment, which is a written examination, project, product, performance or a combination of all of these. The purpose of this external assessment is to test that the knowledge and skills that you have learned have been retained and can be integrated and contextualised. The external assessment determines the grade awarded – A, B or C.

You can study for a National Certificate over a year. Usually, this would be made up of three National Units in vocational subjects. Some National Certificate courses incorporate Scottish Vocational Qualifications (SVQs). They prepare you for employment or more advanced study at the next level. For example, on successful completion, it is possible to move to a Higher National Certificate (HNC).

Group Awards

A Scottish Group Award (SGA) is a programme of study made up of a coherent group of National Courses and Units. They can be completed at all five levels (from Access 2 to Advanced Higher) and are made up of National Courses, National Units and Core Skills that fit together to make a balanced and coherent programme of study, normally lasting a year if you are studying full time and longer if you are studying part time. Untitled or general SGAs are available at all levels. At Intermediate 2 and Higher, there are named SGAs (e.g. an SGA in arts, sciences, business or technology) which are also available. SGAs have been designed to provide progression to further and higher education and employment. There is no overall grade for an SGA; only grades awarded for the individual courses that encompass the SGA.

The five levels in Scotland are:

» **Access**

These are starter courses for young people and adults. There are three access levels. Level 3 is roughly the same level as a Standard Grade Foundation (see page 103). You do not have to sit exams at the end of access courses. Your work is assessed by the class teacher or lecturer.

» **Intermediate 1**

You usually take these courses if you have finished Standard Grade Foundation (or Access 3) level; or you want to take an alternative to Standard Grade General level; or you want to take up a new subject at school or college. Generally, three National Units (blocks of work that usually take 40 hours to finish) plus 40 hours' flexible time make up these courses. This is at level 4 in the SCQF. You can study for these qualifications either in the fifth and sixth years of secondary education or at any time if you are an adult. They are used for a variety of purposes including progression to Highers (see below) in subsequent years.

» **Intermediate 2**

You usually take these courses if you have finished Standard Grade General level; or you want to take an alternative to Standard Grade Credit level; or you want to take up a new subject at school or college. Generally, three National Units (blocks of work that usually take 40 hours to finish) plus 40 hours' flexible time make up these courses. This is at level 5 in the SCQF. You can study for these qualifications either in the fifth and sixth years of secondary education or at any time if you are an adult. They are used for a variety of purposes including progression to Highers in subsequent years.

» **Higher**

You usually take Highers if you have reached Standard Grade Credit (or Intermediate 2) level. You normally need Highers to get into higher education courses (degrees, HNDs and HNCs) at university or college. This is at level 6 in the SCQF. They have pass grades A, B and C.

» **Advanced Higher**

You would usually take Advanced Highers if you have passed Highers. This is at level 7 in the SCQF. Advanced Highers are normally taken at the end of the sixth year of secondary education if you are at school, or at any time if you are an adult. The number of Advanced Highers you can achieve may be affected by the timetabling policy of an individual school, and by the extent to which you decide to broaden your knowledge and skills at Intermediate 2 or Higher levels. These qualifications have three pass grades, which are A, B and C. Advanced Highers are broadly comparable to GCE A-level grades A to C offered in the rest of the UK, but the achievement at GCE A-level grades D and E would not equate to a pass standard for Advanced Higher.

Core Skills

There are five Core Skills, which are communication, IT, numeracy, problem solving and working with others. These are the skills that you will need to get the most out of learning, working and living. They are built into National Units and National Courses, so you do not need to sit extra assessments. However, you can also study them as 'stand-alone' units.

Professional Development Awards (PDAs)

If you have skills and experience in certain areas, you may be eligible to apply to study for a PDA. They are post-experience qualifications, which are available in a number of occupational areas. They are worth considering if you wish to build on your existing skills and experience through working towards a qualification that is recognised nationally and internationally, and which can lead to further qualifications, such as an SVQ or membership of a professional body. They can also help in career development. The awards are related to specific occupational areas and cover subjects such as book-keeping, engineering, PC maintenance, teacher training and care services management. PDAs are awarded at four levels, which are Certificate, Advanced Certificate, Diploma and Advanced Diploma. They are made up of National Units, Higher National Units or SVQ Units, or a combination of these.

National Progression Awards (NPAs)

NPAs are short courses designed to develop and assess your skills and knowledge in vocational areas, such as part-time programmes, whether you are working or unemployed. They are linked to National Occupational Standards, which are the basis of SVQs. They range from Access 2 to Higher, and you can find them at your local further education college.

Scottish Qualifications Certificate (SQC)

The SQC is a lifelong record of your qualifications, which are updated when you add to them. The new certificate has recently been redesigned, into three sections:

1. **Summary of attainment**

   This will list any of the Group Awards, Courses and stand-alone Units that you have achieved since 1994.

2. **Detailed record of attainment**

   This will give more detail about the qualifications achieved since the last certificate was issued.

3. **Profiles**

   This will show your current achievements in Core Skills and SCQF credits.

For more information on these qualifications, contact your employer or the SQA (see *Useful contacts* for details).

Chapter 5

Other learning programmes

Apprenticeships

If you are aged between 16 and 24 and you are not in full-time education, you can apply to become an apprentice. Apprenticeships are a mixture of work-based training and education. You learn on the job, develop skills and knowledge, gain qualifications and earn money at the same time.

Different types of apprenticeships are available in many different occupations and the right one for you will depend on your interests, experience and the opportunities in your area. The occupations come under the headings administration and professional, agriculture and horticulture, construction, customer service, retailing, wholesaling, engineering, finance, insurance and real estate, food and drink, health and beauty, care and public services, hospitality, manufacturing, media and printing, recreation and travel, and transportation.

There are four types of apprenticeship schemes:

1. Young apprenticeships for 14–16 year-olds.
2. Pre-apprenticeships, which are based on the Entry to Employment programme (at level 1) (see page 111).
3. Apprenticeships (at level 2).

4. Advanced apprenticeships (at level 3).

The apprentice programmes have been designed for specific industries by the relevant national training organisation. These programmes define the points for progression, the qualifications to mark the different levels of achievement and your Key Skills.

All apprenticeships include the following basic elements:

» A National Vocational Qualification (NVQ) at the National Qualifications Framework (NQF) level 2, known as the Foundation Modern Apprenticeship in England, and by its original title, National Traineeship, in Wales; or NQF level 3, called the Advanced Modern Apprenticeships in England and the Modern Apprenticeship in Wales.

» Key Skills qualifications, such as working in teams, problem solving, communication and using new technology.

» A Technical Certificate, such as a BTEC or City & Guilds Progression Award.

» Other qualifications or requirements, as specified by particular occupations.

The government plans in future to move away from the three-qualification approach. It plans to put more emphasis on apprentices developing occupational competence, with the necessary underpinning knowledge, skills and qualifications to reward that. In taking this approach the 'technical certificate' will effectively be embedded at apprenticeship, as well as at advanced apprenticeship.

The time to complete an apprenticeship is flexible. It will depend on your ability, the employer's requirements and the chosen occupation, but they usually last between one and three years.

You will get a package of qualifications when you finish your apprenticeship – an NVQ, a Technical Certificate and Key Skills qualifications. An apprentice covers a much wider scope of work than an employee undertaking an NVQ. The qualifications you gain as an apprentice can help you to enter higher education.

WHERE AN APPRENTICESHIP CAN LEAD

You may get a permanent job with the employer or a similar job elsewhere. Also, you could go on to do a foundation degree.

HELP AND ADVICE

Contact the Connexions service or Learn Direct (see *Useful contacts* for details), or look out for apprenticeships advertised by local employers.

Entry to Employment (e2e)

If you feel that you are not ready to cope with work on your own, Entry to Employment (e2e) may be for you. Your e2e programme will be individually designed for you and will help you to prepare for work or an apprenticeship. It will give you an opportunity to try out different jobs or further education.

The scheme is geared to 16 to 18 year-olds, but you may be able to get a place if you are aged up to 24 and if you are not eligible for New Deal (see page 113). Usually, you cannot qualify if you are in employment, but there may be exceptions to this in some circumstances. E2e is facilitated by the Learning and Skills Council and is delivered by learning providers in partnership with Connexions.

You will be learning in three core areas: reading, writing and maths; job search and employability skills; and independent living skills including budgeting. The training is varied – a mixture of classroom-based learning, one-to-one sessions, group activities, online study and work placements. You will be encouraged to work towards a level 1 or entry level qualification. Your e2e programme will last as long as you need it and how often you attend sessions depends on you; the scheme is tailored to suit your needs and your choices determine how you progress. Attendance will vary from 16 hours up to 40 hours a week, but this will depend on your learning capacity, aspirations, needs and progression choices.

You can apply for an Education Maintenance Allowance (see Chapter 7). You can also get bonuses for starting the programme and for achievements, such as completing what is called an Individual Activity Plan or gaining a qualification.

WHERE DOES IT LEAD?

E2e helps you progress towards an apprenticeship, further vocational learning opportunities or a job.

Note: At the time of writing this book, the scheme does not exist in Scotland, although there is a similar scheme (called Activate) for school leavers in certain areas.

HELP AND ADVICE

Contact Connexions or Learn Direct. If you are at school, it may also be able to help. Specific information on e2e can be found at www.dfes.gov.uk.

The Prince's Trust

If you have struggled at school, the Prince's Trust may be able to help you to turn things around and to get your life back on track. It can offer a range of opportunities, including training, help with CVs, working on community projects (including projects abroad), assisting with personal development, business start-up support, mentoring and advice. You could spend two to three weeks helping on a community project in Europe. You may also be able to get a development award of £50 to 500 through the trust, to help you get into work, training or education.

To be eligible, you must be between 14 and 30. In most cases you also have to be unemployed, or someone who left school with few or no qualifications. You will also be eligible if you are in care, leaving care, or if you are an ex-offender.

If you are 16 to 25, you can apply to get on one of the Prince's Trust team programmes, called 'Team'. Through these programmes you can achieve qualifications away from a classroom environment. The qualifications available are City & Guilds qualifications – The Certificate in Personal, Teamwork and Community Skills or the Qualifications and Curriculum Authority's (QCA) Key Skill Units in England, Wales and Northern Ireland, or the Scottish Vocational Qualifications (SVQ) Core Skill Units in Scotland. Team is a 12-week personal development programme that helps build confidence and improve employability. While you are on a programme, you will compile a portfolio of work, developing skills such as teamwork and communications. You will have the chance to work on a community project of your choosing and get two weeks' work experience, maybe at a professional football or cricket club, if you wish to do so. You will learn practical skills that help you in a job and in life, and receive careers advice including help with your CV and looking for a job.

It is also possible to get on a programme if you are employed, if your employer is prepared to nominate you. You will spend 20 days of the programme with unemployed people and you will be able to work on a project to help a community. The whole idea is to give you valuable skills in areas such as communication and planning, plus it enables you to develop confidence, focus, motivation and management skills to help you when you return to the workplace.

Would you be interested in leading a team of unemployed young people on a programme? You could apply to be seconded by your employer to a project where you can do this. This will help you gain facilitation skills, develop management ability, learn how to motivate and inspire a team and help young people who are facing barriers in life.

For more information, log on to the Prince's Trust website (see *Useful contacts* for details).

New Deal and other Jobcentre Plus programmes

Your local Jobcentre Plus office will offer a number of services and programmes to help you find a way to improve your skills and job prospects. Some staff specialise in certain areas such as the over 50s, the under 25s and disabled people. An adviser at your local Jobcentre Plus office can discuss the type of work you want and training opportunities that may be available.

There is a government programme called New Deal with different schemes for certain groups of people. Everyone on New Deal gets a personal adviser who is their point of contact throughout the programme. The personal adviser takes the time to understand you – your experiences, interests and goals – so a plan can be prepared to get you into a suitable job. As part of the New Deal training scheme, you can choose the 'education and training' option. If you choose this option, you will usually get your course costs paid for and you can get help with related costs, such as books, transport, childcare, etc.

HELP AND ADVICE

If you have any questions about New Deal, contact your local Jobcentre Plus office or call 0845 606 2626, 7am to 11pm, seven days a week. The textphone service for deaf and hearing impaired people is 0845 606 0680.

Here is an outline of the various schemes available:

» **Work Trial**

A Work Trial gives you the opportunity to try out in an actual job vacancy with an employer. It will give you the chance to show an employer that you are the right person to fill a job. You will also continue to receive benefits and you could be paid travel and meal expenses too. You will normally be eligible for a Work Trial if you are aged 25 years or over and have been unemployed for six months or more (although there are some exceptions to this).

During a Work Trial you will get the chance to try out a job for up to 15 working days and show an employer that you are the right person to fill it. You will continue to receive any benefits you are entitled to (e.g. Jobseeker's Allowance, Incapacity Benefit, Income Support), and you will be paid travel expenses of up to £10 per day and meal expenses of up to £3 per day.

» **Employment on Trial**

Employment on Trial helps give you the confidence to start a new job, even if you are not sure if it will work out. This is because you will not jeopardise your benefit if you have to leave the job, as long as you have given it a fair try. To be eligible, you must stay in the job for over four weeks, but not more than 12 weeks, and have worked for at least 16 hours in each week. You must also have been out of work or full-time education for at least 13 weeks before the job starts. Of course, the Jobcentre Plus office hopes that the job will work out so that you do not have to sign on again.

» **Pathways to Work**

In some areas of the country, if you get Incapacity Benefit or Income Support on health grounds, Pathways to Work could help you return to work. You will get tailored support from a personal adviser, access to job support and NHS rehabilitation and you may also be entitled to Return to Work Credit. If you would like to volunteer to participate in Pathways to Work, you must check with your local Jobcentre Plus office, Jobcentre or Social Security office in your area.

Pathways to Work has been developed to provide greater support to help people claiming Incapacity Benefit back into, or closer to, the labour market. As part of this scheme the Condition Management Programme (CMP) has been developed in partnership with the National Health Service (NHS). CMP is designed to help people understand and manage their health condition in a work environment.

Return to Work Credit is a payment of £40 a week for people starting work who work at least 16 hours a week and earn no more than £15,000 per year. Anyone wishing to apply has to have been receiving Incapacity Benefit (including Statutory Sick

Pay) for 13 weeks immediately prior to starting work. It is payable for up to 52 weeks.

» New Deal for Young People (NDYP)

If you are aged between 18 and 24 and have had a continuous claim to Jobseeker's Allowance for six months or more, then you must take part in this programme, otherwise you can have your Jobseeker's Allowance withdrawn.

The aim of NDYP is to improve your chances of finding and keeping a job. You will receive the continued help and support from a New Deal personal adviser, whose main aim is to help you review your situation, take the skills and experience you may have already and build on them to create better opportunities for work. In some cases you may be invited to join the programme even though you have been on Jobseeker's Allowance for less than six months, if both you and your personal adviser decide that this is the best course of action for you.

To begin with there is a Gateway stage, which comprises informal discussions and some training on preparing CVs and job hunting. Following this, if you are still claiming Jobseeker's Allowance, there will be the Option stage, which is a period of intensive support to meet your specific needs. This period may include work experience placement in a field you are interested in, which can help you develop your skills. You will receive a training allowance equivalent to your Jobseeker's Allowance and you may also receive a top-up payment of £15.38 per week.

» New Deal 25 plus (ND25 plus)

If you are aged 25 or over and have had either a continuous claim to Jobseeker's Allowance for 18 months or have been claiming Jobseeker's Allowance for 18 out of 21 months, then ND25 plus is relevant to you. Again, this is a mandatory programme. In some cases you may be invited to join the programme earlier than 18 months if both you and the New Deal personal adviser decide that this is the best course of action for you to take.

Its aim and format is the same as for NDYP. It gives you a chance to take another look at your situation, take the skills and experience you may have already and build on them to create better opportunities for work.

» New Deal 50 plus (ND50 plus)

If you are 50 or over, ND50 plus offers support and advice on finding employment. It also offers training and help if you have found it difficult to get a job or work that pays a decent wage. Again, the aim and format is the same as for NDYP.

You are eligible for this programme if you or your partner receive, or have been receiving, any one or more of the following benefits for at least six months: Pension Credit, Income Support, Jobseeker's Allowance, Incapacity Benefit and Severe Disablement Allowance.

» New Deal for Lone Parents (NDLP)

You can join NDLP if you are bringing up children as a lone parent, if your youngest child is under 16 years old and you are not working, or you are working less than 16 hours per week.

This is a voluntary programme specifically designed to help lone parents into work. It offers a package of support to help you move towards a more secure future for you and your children.

If you choose to take advantage of what is available by joining the scheme, a personal adviser will take you through the steps to help you find and apply for jobs. The aim and format is the same as for NDYP. Your adviser will also offer practical advice and help about finding childcare and training. He will also be able to advise you on how your benefits will be affected when you start work and he will help you apply for any in-work benefits or tax credits.

» New Deal for Partners (NDP)

If your partner is claiming benefit for you, you
NDP programme and get a whole range
programme is voluntary so you can choose wh

want to take part. It is available to partners of people claiming any of the following benefits: Jobseeker's Allowance, Income Support, Incapacity Benefit, Carer's Allowance, Severe Disablement Benefit and Pension Credit. You can also join if your partner gets Pension Credit and you are working less than 24 hours a week, or if you or your partner get Working Tax Credit and you are working less than 16 hours a week.

If you join NDP, you will work with a personal adviser, who is there to talk you through your situation, give advice and help you to find the right support you need. The aim and format is the same as for NDYP. He will provide advice on training courses and education so that you can learn new skills, as well as possible jobs. He will also help with the cost of childcare and fares when you are attending training courses, meetings and job interviews, and work out what you need to earn for your family to be better off, including any in-work benefits that you may be entitled to.

» New Deal for Musicians (NDfM)

NDfM is intended to help aspiring unemployed musicians attain a sustainable career in the music industry, as either artists under contract or self-employed artists within the music industry. All genres of music are catered for on NDfM – rock/pop, dance, jazz, blues, country and western, folk, classical and even DJs. It does not directly provide musical tuition, which is provided by other formal training routes; rather it provides advice and guidance on the business aspects of work in the music industry.

NDfM is also part of the NDYP and ND25 plus, both of which are mandatory programmes. Under this scheme the extra support you can receive at the Option stage (see *New Deal for Young People (NDYP)* on page 116) may be through music industry providers, who provide one-to-one support through industry experts.

» New Deal for Disabled People (NDDP)

See Chapter 8 for more information.

» **The Training for Work Programme (Scotland only)**

In Scotland there is also the Training for Work Programme. You are eligible if you are 25 or over and are claiming certain benefits for 26 weeks, although early entry is possible in some cases. It is a voluntary training programme to help unemployed and disadvantaged adults improve their work-related skills and increase their chances of getting a job.

You can receive a weekly allowance equal to your benefits plus £10 and help towards certain travel expenses.

Training for Work is managed and delivered by Scottish Enterprise and Highlands and Islands Enterprise through their network of Local Enterprise Companies and they also work closely with Jobcentre Plus.

You can find out more about Training for Work at your local Jobcentre or through the Local Enterprise Company in your area. See www.scottish-enterprise.com/sedotcom_home/about_se/local_enterprise_companies.htm for more information.

Ruskin College

Ruskin College is included here as it is unusual in that it specialises in providing educational opportunities for adults with few or no qualifications. The college's aim is to change the lives of those who need a second chance in education. Ruskin welcomes students who not only want to develop themselves but also want to put something back into society.

If you are someone who was unable to study up to now due to financial, personal or social obstacles, and you are able to move to Oxford to take up a course, Ruskin may be worth considering. To help fund your place, apart from the sources listed in Chapter 8, there are a number of scholarships you can apply for, although many of them are only available if you are a member of a trade union or the Labour Party. The college offers a range of courses in the informal setting of a small residential college. According to its website, the college will support its students through the emotional and personal difficulties of learning while demonstrating that they 'give of their best'. See *Useful contacts* for details.

The 'Learning through Work' scheme

The 'Learning through Work' scheme can enable you to achieve a university qualification while you work. Learn Direct has entered into a partnership with certain universities and colleges to offer a university course to be tailored precisely to your needs.

A number of recognised higher education qualifications are offered, ranging from undergraduate certificates, Honours degrees and even postgraduate degrees and doctorates. Shorter programmes are available and count as credits within the university system. Training programmes include work-based activities, courses, distance learning modules, in-house training and practical research, or a mixture of all of these methods. The scheme builds on your existing learning, takes account of your work context and provides a structure so that you can plan for new learning that is specific to you as an individual. University advisers will help you turn your ideas into a learning programme.

Learning through Work requires you to be responsible for your managing your own learning. This does not mean that you are on your own. Help and guidance is provided by means of handbooks and guides, internet discussion boards and email. You may be able to learn with colleagues. Learning through Work provides you with support and guidance to help you develop the knowledge and skills necessary to design a programme that is unique and meaningful to you, to identify your future learning needs and to plan for your personal, professional and career development.

The participating universities are the University of Chester, the University of Derby, the University of Central Lancashire (in Preston), Northumbria University, the University of Northampton, the University of the West of England (in Bristol) and Staffordshire University.

HELP AND ADVICE

Talk to your employer or your company's human resources department if it has one. It may already participate in this scheme, but if it does not, you could encourage the company to do so. For more information, contact Learn Direct. Its website contains information and exercises to help you decide if Learning through Work is right for you. Also log on to the Learning through Work website (see *Useful contacts* for details). The universities themselves can also give guidance on fees and they can be contacted through this site.

The Foyer scheme

If you are homeless or with no settled home, or if you are about to leave care, you may find it of assistance to get in touch with a Foyer near you. The UK Foyer network exists to support you if you are a homeless 16 to 25 year-old and it gives you a chance to realise your full potential.

It enables you to escape the 'no-home-no-job no-home' cycle by providing a stable and secure community in which you can gradually learn to become independent. The Foyer will provide temporary accommodation, personal support and help with motivation, plus some training to help you live independently and gain some basic skills. It will also go on to help you with job hunting by finding other training and education which will help you get a better job. Foyer will also help you find permanent accommodation, and you will receive ongoing support when you move on.

The scheme is overseen by the Foyer Federation, which gives a voice to 134 local Foyers across the UK, and to the 10,000 disadvantaged young people with whom it works each year. It provides a forum for sharing best practice and accessing funding, training and a range of support, while the Foyer Accreditation Scheme ensures the quality and consistency of Foyer services. Log on to its website for more information (see *Useful contacts* for details).

Residential training for disabled adults

If you are disabled and there is no suitable training locally for you, there is a scheme called 'residential training for disabled adults'. This is designed to help long-term unemployed disabled people secure and maintain jobs or self-employment. The programme is provided when there are no suitable alternative programmes available locally.

The training takes place in a residential setting in accessible buildings. Staff members with specialist knowledge of disability issues teach the courses. The programme is tailored to meet your training needs through a combination of guidance, work experience, vocational (work-based) training and qualifications.

To be eligible, you have to be over 18 with a physical and/or sensory disability or learning difficulty, be unemployed and have the potential to take up employment, including supported employment. You will receive an allowance during your training and your residential costs, which can also include some travel costs, will be paid for.

Courses vary from college to college, with over 50 courses of vocational training available through the programme. Many lead to NVQs. They include administration, audio-visual, construction trades, catering, cycle mechanics, decorating, electronics, engineering, horticulture, information technology, leisure, tourism and travel, recording studio technicians, retail, tele-working and vehicle refinishing. The length of courses will vary according to your needs, but they will not exceed 52 weeks. Some training programmes are specifically designed for people with a hearing or visual impairment.

There are ten specialist course providers located throughout England. To apply for residential training, you should contact your Disability Employment Adviser (DEA) at your local Jobcentre Plus office or Jobcentre and he will explore the options available to you. He can also give you information about the benefits you may receive while you are on the programme.

You can get further information about residential training from the Residential Training Unit (see *Useful contacts* for details).

Chapter 6

Where to study

Home study

Home study is possible for many courses and distance learning usually requires study from home (see Chapter 2). You may be sent course materials by post or online and you can also receive support from a tutor via phone, email or post.

Correspondence courses and home study are the same as distance learning. On an open learning course (see Chapter 2) you will probably have a mixture of study methods, including studying at home, using a resource centre and face-to-face tuition. With other types of courses you can partly study at home when you are completing homework and assignments.

Open and distance learning courses are mostly provided by universities, colleges and private companies. Details of providers are available from Learn Direct (see *Useful contacts* for details). Before enrolling, check if the course provider is accredited and that it is offering the qualification you want at the appropriate level.

The Open and Distance Learning Quality Council (ODLQC) is an independent body that inspects course providers and assesses whether their quality standards are being met. Most approved course providers show the ODLQC accreditation logo on their promotional material. The ODLQC website (see *Useful contacts* for details) lists its accredited colleges, the courses you can study, and it has more general information and advice on open and distance learning.

There is also the Association of British Correspondence Colleges (see *Useful contacts* for details), which is a trade association whose members adhere to a code of ethics that maintain quality. If a course provider uses another organisation's accreditation logo on its course materials, check that it is a reputable and independent organisation that inspects course providers.

There are many non-accredited course providers. If a course provider is not accredited by one of these organisations, you will have to assess the quality of its courses yourself. You should get answers to the following questions:

» Does the course lead to a recognised qualification (if you need one)?

» Has the course provider got a customer satisfaction or refund policy? You may want to quit the course due to a change in your personal circumstances.

» Is there a guaranteed level of tutor support? Is it via phone, email or face-to-face?

» Will the provider send you an example of the course materials?

» Will the provider put you in touch with other people who have completed the course?

» Is the course at the right level? If not, get some advice and guidance or speak to the course tutor.

» Do you need to attend tutorials, face-to-face tuition and examinations? If so, how often?

» Is the course available through other providers? Shop around to see if you can get a better deal.

» How much will it all cost in total? In addition to the course fee, you may have to pay for an enrolment fee, books, equipment, examination costs, internet usage, travel and accommodation.

» Does the course have any time restrictions? Although many distance learning courses are open-ended and you learn at your own pace, some have time limits.

Increasingly courses are delivered online (see *E-learning* in Chapter 2). Many are run by the government agency Learn Direct. It has a selection of courses that you can buy online and begin learning straight away, mostly in the fields of information technology (IT), languages, business and management courses and Skills for Life (numeracy and literacy skills).

If you do not want to use course providers, you can learn informally at home by using the following:

» **Books**

There are many 'how to' books where you can learn anything from computer skills to DIY.

» **Audio tapes and CDs**

Many people learn languages using this method, although other common topics are management skills and personal development.

» **Home computer**

You can learn computer skills with a tuition manual, an on-screen tutorial or via the internet.

» **TV and radio**

The BBC's Learning Zone (www.bbc.co.uk/learningzone) is a good site to use.

These options are different from structured courses because they do not usually lead to formal qualifications and there is no tutor support. But this method may suit you if you want to get used to studying a particular subject.

Learn Direct centre

Learn Direct is a national training provider and learning information and advice service. Its courses are internet based, but as well as accessing them from your home or work, you can, if you prefer, use one of the many Learn Direct centres around the country.

Learn Direct's flexible learning is available to you if you want to improve your existing skills or to learn new ones, and to employers looking for an innovative way to develop the skills of their workforce.

More than 550 different courses are offered covering a range of subjects, including management, IT, Skills for Life and languages, at all levels. Learn Direct's staff will be on hand to guide you through your learning step by step, whether or not you have had any previous experience of studying the subject. You will find them in sports clubs, leisure and community centres, churches, libraries, on university campuses and even some railway stations. They are there to help you get started, no matter when and where you decide to learn.

Facilities range from crèches, cafés, parking, free internet access, lending libraries, games rooms and desktop publishing facilities. The facilities vary from centre to centre so when you arrive check what they have to offer or give them a ring beforehand. To find out the most convenient centres for you, or for further information, log on to the Learn Direct or Learn Direct Scotland websites or call their helplines (see *Useful contacts*).

Local authority adult education centre

Whether you want to learn more about a subject to improve your job prospects or you just enjoy learning, local authority adult education centres offer a wide range of learning opportunities at a level to suit you. Their courses will enable you to increase your skills and knowledge, gain a qualification, open new doors at work and in life, and gain confidence to progress further. Courses are run as daytime or evening classes.

Contact your local education authority (i.e. your local council) for details of what is available in your area. Many local authorities are members of the National Institute of Adult Continuing Education (NIACE), and its website (see *Useful contacts*) may also be helpful. There is an alphabetical list of corporate members so you can search for the place you live.

Sixth form college

In some areas of England, Wales and Northern Ireland if you are between 16 and 18, you can study during the day at a sixth form college to complete further education qualifications, such as GCE A-levels and vocational qualifications, such as BTECs and OCR Nationals (see Chapter 4).

Sixth form colleges usually exist as an alternative to school and students study there for two years (known as Years 12 and 13 or 'lower sixth' and 'upper sixth'). After completing college, students generally pass on to university, or go straight to employment.

There are currently about 100 sixth form colleges in operation in England and Wales. Most perform extremely well in national examination league tables. In addition, they offer a broader range of courses at a lower cost per student than most school sixth forms.

Colleges for the most part do not charge full-time daytime students. However, it may be possible to attend evening classes in certain subjects, in which case you may be charged fees for tuition and exams.

For further information on whether there are any sixth form colleges near you, contact your school, the Connexions service or the Learning and Skills Council (see *Useful contacts*). The college or its website will be able to provide you with further information, including a prospectus on the facilities and courses it offers. It will also have open days so that you can go along and see what is available and discuss any issues you have with the college.

Further education (FE) college

Further education (FE) colleges are usually larger than sixth form colleges although what they provide does vary a lot, depending on what else is on offer locally. If most local schools have sixth forms, or there are local sixth form colleges, the FE college may specialise in academic or vocational subjects which closely link to the needs of commerce or industry. These could include subjects such as art, agriculture or technology, many of which can lead to university entry.

In areas where the FE college is the only, or the main, option after 16, it will offer everything you could get in a school sixth form or sixth form college. Some FE colleges will have more than one site and some will have separate 'sixth form centres'. Although most students at FE colleges are over 16, all colleges will have part-time and adult students. Some colleges may also offer higher education courses, such as Higher National Diplomas (HNDs) and bachelor's degrees.

The departments of some colleges are also classified as Centres of Vocational Excellence (CoVEs). CoVEs excel in a particular area of vocational learning which meets the skill needs of employers, either locally or within a region, in subjects such as construction, engineering, agriculture and hospitality. Qualifications include Skills for Life, BTECs and OCR Nationals, NVQ levels 1 to 4, and foundation degrees.

For further information on the nearest FE college near you, contact your school, the Connexions service or the Learning and Skills Council. The college or its website will be able to provide you with further information, including a prospectus on the facilities and courses available. It will also have open days so that you can go along and see what is on offer and discuss any issues you have with the college.

Commercial training provider

There are thousands of commercial training providers and most of them will provide training in particular subject areas. To find one, you will need to shop around locally and the Connexions service (if you are under 19) may advise. Alternatively, you could speak to your local library, look in the *Yellow Pages* or the phone book, or go online to find a provider to suit your needs. In order to get the best deal, it is advisable to ask the questions listed on page 124.

If you are looking for vocational training, trade associations may be able to recommend approved private training providers or offer tips on finding reputable ones. Sometimes, they even offer their own training courses. You may be able to find a contact for a relevant trade association by using the Contacts Directory on the Business Link website (see *Useful contacts*). Alternatively, you could approach a relevant professional body for information about training provision.

The training courses and information offered by these organisations, or recommended by them, will be less sector specific and more general; for example, relating to exporting or accounting. They often have the advantage of professional recognition. This is particularly the case if the training is to be provided as part of a Continuing Professional Development programme (see the Introduction for more information).

If you are employed, your employer may use a commercial training provider to train you in the workplace.

You can also contact the Sector Skills Councils (SSCs), if the training you need is related to a particular occupation. These are government-licensed independent organisations which bring together employers, trade unions and professional bodies. Their aim is to identify and tackle skill shortages and gaps by sector. The SSCs are outlined in Chapter 9 and their addresses are listed in *Useful contacts*.

Workplace training

Training provided within the workplace varies from employer to employer. Some may provide a full range with all sorts of options to help you develop your career, others will outsource their training to outside companies, and others may provide nothing at all. Some will put more emphasis on on-the-job training or they may meet your expenses for training outside the company (see the Introduction, *Test the employer* on page xix). Talk to your human resources department, if there is one, or your boss or line manager. If you cannot persuade your employer to provide training, you may have to consider changing your job or taking a course in your own time.

Some employers will have links with Learn Direct Business – the business arm of the government agency Learn Direct. It has been developed by University for Industry (Ufi) to inspire existing learners to develop their skills further, win over new and excluded learners, and transform the accessibility of learning in everyday life and work. The flexibility of e-learning, coupled with the Learn Direct portfolio of business-focused courses, means that Ufi has something to offer employers of all sizes, whether from the private, voluntary or public sector. As every employer is different, Ufi has developed separate approaches to working with small businesses, SSCs and large employers, from all sectors, to address their specific needs.

You can access Learn Direct courses at any stage in your working life, starting at a level and working at a pace that suits you. See Chapter 4, *Working towards a qualification with Learn Direct* on page 73. The 'Learning through Work' scheme is one of the Learn Direct programmes that may appeal to you (see Chapter 5).

For further information about Ufi's work with employers, go to www.learndirect-business.co.uk.

Help from trade unions

If you are a member of a trade union, you may be able to get help with your training needs. If you are employed and there is a trade union in your workplace which is relevant to your job, you may want to consider joining. Most unions are very active in encouraging employers to take workplace learning seriously. They may be prepared to act on your behalf to help you get the training opportunities you need.

Some employers work with unions to offer Return to Learn schemes. An example is UNISON's Return to Learn programme, which has been running since 1989. It offers educational opportunities to union members who missed out in the education system. Return to Learn is provided through the union's Open College, which adopts a 'passport' approach to learning, giving all members access to flexible learning at the appropriate level. The union has also developed a Return to Learn Partnership, where employers commit themselves to working with the union to improve education and training.

The Return to Learn programme also provides a stepping stone into higher education. Students gain admission to university either through an accumulation of Return to Learn credits or via a one-year union access course.

Trade unions may also provide, or arrange, their own training in such areas as union representation, health and safety representation, pension scheme trusteeship, as well as teaching you to be a learning representative, an equality representative, a union professional or a trade union tutor. Usually, no previous educational qualifications are required. Of course, you would usually only be able to undertake this kind of course if you were committed to having a role in the union. Even so, it will improve your skills and confidence as well. You may be able to use the union's own learning facilities, or the courses may be provided at a local college. If your employer officially recognises the union in the workplace, you have the right to paid leave to take up such courses.

The Trades Union Congress (TUC) has established 'unionlearn' to help unions develop training, and to help them broker learning opportunities for their members, provide phone and online advice services, secure the best courses to meet learners' needs and regulate quality standards. Unionlearn also strives to keep workplace learning on the national agenda, identifies and shares good practice, promotes learning agreements, supports union members on learning and skills bodies, and helps shape sector skills agreements by working on SSCs. These councils exist to identify and tackle skill shortages and gaps in each occupational sector.

The TUC also runs National Open College Network (NOCN) accredited programmes delivered locally through dedicated TUC units in 76 FE colleges across the UK. All course materials are designed, developed and provided by the TUC and tutors are recruited for their expertise in trade unionism and the world of work.

In addition, the General Federation of Trade Unions (GFTU) administers the GFTU Educational Trust, through which it offers a full programme of trade union education courses. They cover most areas of interest to trade unionists including industrial relations, health and safety, IT and equality and diversity. These courses are held in different venues around the country and they are aimed at both trade union representatives and members.

The GFTU Educational Trust is also involved in running various projects that are funded by various government departments and the European Union. At the moment these include the Union Learning Fund, the Pensions Education Fund and the Development Awareness Fund. Each year it aims to provide high-quality and varied learning opportunities that are delivered in a relaxed and informal environment.

HELP AND ADVICE

Most union services are only available to members. If you are a member, or wish to join a union in your workplace, contact the learning representative of the union, or speak to another union representative. You can also contact the union's branch or head office.

For more information on TUC education and training courses, go to www.unionlearn.org.uk and the General Federation of Trade Unions (GFTU) website (see *Useful contacts* for details).

University

A university is an institution of higher education and research which grants academic degrees at all levels (bachelor, master and doctorate) in a variety of subjects. A university provides both higher and postgraduate education.

There are many around the UK, especially as 46 new ones were created in 1992 from former polytechnics and higher education institutions. Anybody, regardless of their age and background, can go to university and they go for different reasons. You may want to continue your education after you have finished your A-levels or you may want to improve your skills if you are thinking of a change of career. Maybe you just want to study something you are interested in.

At university you will be able to work towards a certificate, diploma or bachelor's degree qualification. Most full-time degree courses will take three to four years to complete, or longer if you are studying part time.

With most universities you will need to apply for entry via the Universities and Colleges Admissions Service (UCAS). It operates a system called the 'UCAS Tariff'. If you have any qualification at level 3 on the National Qualifications Framework, you can earn points on the Tariff for entry into higher education. Different courses will ask for a different number of points (see Chapter 4 on bachelor's degrees).

If the university is regarded as particularly high status (e.g. Oxford or Cambridge) or a leader in your chosen subject area, the entry qualifications will be higher grades at A-level and there may be a separate entry examination or other form of assessment. To find out entrance requirements for a particular course, you can do a search on the UCAS website (see *Useful contacts)* or read the course prospectus – most are now available online.Having said this, in some cases if you are a mature student, the university may be more flexible, especially if you can show your commitment to study and learning (some recent experience of study will help further). It will also help your case if you can show particular interest and some knowledge of the subject you want to study.

For information on all aspects of the applications process for full-time undergraduate courses at universities and colleges, contact UCAS. Also, any university you are interested in will be able to provide you with further information, including a prospectus on its facilities and courses it offers. It will also have open days so that you can go along and see what is available and to discuss any issues you have with the university. Log on to its website. At every university there will be trained careers advisers who will be able to advise you about all the different degrees, certificates and diploma qualifications you will be able to take.

There are many good websites which also may be able to help; for example:

» www.opendays.com provides information on open days and has contact details for over 400 universities and colleges in the UK.

» HERO (Higher Education and Research Opportunities in the United Kingdom) is the national portal for higher education in the UK (see *Useful contacts*).

» You can also look at the Connexions website (see *Useful contacts*). (Although it is geared to those under the age of 19, most of it will be relevant, whatever your age.)

» The Learn Direct website (see *Useful contacts*).

» The Careers Gateway (www.careers-gateway.co.uk).

For a young person, in particular, it is often regarded as a bigger step to go to university because you may have to live away from home to go to the place of your choosing, so there could be other issues you may have to resolve, such as finding accommodation and settling into a new town. Do not forget, though, that there may be a suitable university within travelling distance from your home, or you may have the option of part-time study so you can more easily maintain other commitments, such as family and work, as well. Note that the Open University is Britain's sole distance-learning university – see Chapter 2, *The Open University* on page 44.

Chapter 7

Financing your learning

You know your goal and have decided on a course. You are ready to take the leap. Maybe now you are wondering how you will fund the course or what you will live on.

Learning always costs something, whether you are planning to do a full-time, part-time or self-study course. You might have to pay course fees or adjust your household budget so you have enough to live on. Full-time courses will probably have the most impact on your finances. However, if you do not learn new skills, this can cost you even more in the long run. It is important that you keep your skills up to date to keep up with changes in the workplace.

When you are considering finance, take into account extra expenses such as books, equipment, travel costs, field trips, registration and exam fees. Also, have a good look at your household finances. Think about your outgoings, such as your mortgage or rent, bills and loans. Can you reduce these, maybe on a temporary basis?

Here is a list of living costs. These will be higher if you live away from home, and higher still if you live away from home and study in London:

» Food
» Household bills – gas, electricity, water rates, phone, TV licence, contents insurance (some of these are covered by rent in halls of residence)

» Clothes

» Travel

» Socialising

» Leisure and sport

» Study costs, such as books, materials and field trips for your course

The website of the National Union of Students (NUS) (see *Useful contacts*) has more useful information on living costs.

Sources of advice

The best advice is that you research all possible sources of funding. The funding system for further education, in particular, can be complex, and what you are entitled to will depend upon your circumstances and which subject, and level, you are studying. Funding may be from a public body (like an education authority), a private organisation (like a bank) or a charitable organisation. You may qualify for extra help if you have children or adult dependants, or have a disability or specific learning difficulty.

The Educational Grants Advisory Service (EGAS) provides information and advice on all funding for post-16 education. It advises on standard sources of funding, such as grants, loans, bursaries and hardship funds. It also advises on non-standard funding, such as educational trusts and charities. If you fill in a questionnaire, EGAS can check which funding you may be eligible for and it will send you the details. You can fill in the questionnaire online on the EGAS website or you can get advice by calling its helpline (see *Useful contacts* for details).

Also, you may still qualify for welfare benefits if you are studying full or part time, so this can help you with your living expenses.

Here are some websites which will provide you with information:

» Connexions (see *Useful contacts*), if you are under 19.

» Learn Direct (see *Useful contacts*), if you are over 19.

» Student Finance Direct is the main government site to help you find out more about financial support in higher education. The site includes online applications. Log on to www.studentfinance direct.co.uk.

» Support4Learning (www.support4learning.org.uk/money) is another good source of information, with details on a wide range of support services, grants, bursaries and awards.

» The website www.direct.gov.uk has a lot of information about the types of financial help that is available for students. Visit www.direct.gov.uk/en/EducationAndLearning. Also, this site has another section to introduce you to the welfare benefits and tax credits to which you may be entitled. See www.direct.gov. uk/en/MoneyTaxAndBenefits/index.htm.

» The Citizens Advice Bureau (CAB) service can also advise on student finance welfare benefits. Either drop in to your local CAB or use www.adviceguide.org.uk. To find your nearest CAB, log on to www.citizensadvice.org.uk.

If you need help with childcare costs while you study, consider Learner Support Funds (see page 153) or Parents' Learning Allowance (see page 164).

Education Maintenance Allowance (EMA)

You can claim EMA if you are aged 16, 17 or 18. It is a weekly payment which is as an incentive for you to stay on in education once you are 16.

It is paid directly to you if you continue in learning after you reach statutory school leaving age. You have to be undertaking full-time education at a school or college, or join an approved training course with an e2e programme (funded by the Learning and Skills Council (LSC)), or become an apprentice which involves at least 12 hours of guided learning per week (see Chapter 5). This requirement includes a wide range of courses up to and including level 3 of the National

Qualifications Framework (NQF), such as AS/A2, GCSEs, General National Vocational Qualifications (GNVQs), National Vocational Qualifications (NVQs) and other vocational qualifications.

You can get £10, £20 or £30 a week, depending on your household income in the previous tax year (i.e. your parents' income and any income you may receive). For example, if you are claiming between April 2007 and March 2008, your household income has to have been under £30,810 during tax year 20006/07 to qualify. However, these figures will be higher in some circumstances (e.g. if you have a dependant living with you). Also, they may be slightly increased overall from March 2009.

EMA does not affect other welfare benefits paid to parents or carers, or students. You will receive a payment every week of your course, as long as you turn up to your classes. From time to time, you may also qualify for bonus payments. If your learning programme lasts over two years, these payments could be worth up to £500. To get these, you will need to meet specific goals agreed between you and your school, college or provider, demonstrating real progress and commitment to your learning programme. To find out how much your bonus payments could be, contact your school, college or learning provider.

For further information on the EMA, contact Connexions (see *Useful contacts*) or visit the EMA website at www.dfes.gov. uk/financialhelp/ema. You can also speak to someone over the phone on EMA's helpline on 0808 101 6219. The EMA Young Person's leaflet should be available at your school or college. You can also download a PDF from the EMA website or call 0845 60 222 60 to request a copy (ref LSC-P-NAT-060002).

Career Development Loan (CDL)

CDL is a deferred repayment bank loan to help you pay for work-related learning or education. You can borrow between £300 and £8,000 to fund up to two years of learning plus (if relevant) up to one year's practical work experience where it forms part of the course. You might consider a CDL if you need to develop a skill and you cannot get funding for the course.

The LSC pays the interest on your loan while you are learning, and for up to one month afterwards. You then repay the loan to the bank over an agreed period at a fixed rate of interest. Repayments should start when you have finished the course. If you claim welfare benefits or do not go straight into work, you may be given more time before starting the repayments.

CDLs are available through Barclays Bank, the Co-operative and the Royal Bank of Scotland.

To be eligible, you must be aged 18 or over and you must intend to learn in England, Scotland or Wales. Also, you must intend to work in the European Union, Iceland, Norway or Liechtenstein after you have finished your course. You can be employed, unemployed or self-employed, provided you have insufficient savings to pay for the course yourself. The loan may be allowed for a course of up to two years (with an extra year if a work placement is included). If the course is over two years, the loan will usually cover the last two years only.

You can use a CDL for most full-time, part-time or distance learning courses as long as they are vocational (leads to an occupation, trade or profession). Examples include NVQs, City & Guilds courses and vocational postgraduate courses. The loan can cover not only course fees, but other course costs (such as childcare, travel and equipment) and living expenses. You cannot use a CDL for anything you are receiving other funding to cover. This includes local education authority (LEA) awards, National Health Service (NHS) bursaries, money from employers or if you have enough money to fund the study yourself.

Log on to www.direct.gov.uk for more information.

Adult Learning Grant (ALG)

ALG is a means-tested grant, paid weekly during term time if you are studying, or about to study, full-time for a first level 2 (five GCSEs or equivalent) or level 3 qualification (two A-levels or equivalent). You can only qualify if you do not already have a qualification at level 3 or higher (see Chapter 3 for more information on the levels of the NQF).

The grant is only available to learners in full-time learning who have lived in England during the three years before the course started. The definition of full-time learning is full-time, full year learning (i.e. at least 450 guided learning hours in any 12-month period) or full-time, part year learning (i.e. at least 150 guided learning hours per term). This usually means that you have to be studying for at least 12 hours per week.

Normally, the grant will be paid for up to two years, but this can be extended if you are studying for a first full level 2 and then immediately progressing to a first full level 3 and you expect to complete your learning within a maximum of three years. You will get the payments weekly during term time, as long as your course attendance is satisfactory.

To be eligible, you must be aged 19 or over. You can be aged 18, but the earliest date you can apply is one month before your 19th birthday. You can also apply on or after reaching the age of 19. If you were receiving the EMA and are continuing study to attain your first full level 2 or first full level 3 course, you will qualify to receive ALG for another year, subject to your meeting all the eligibility criteria.

You can get £10, £20 or £30 a week, depending on your annual household income in the previous tax year. This would include your partner's or spouse's income if you live with him. For example, if you are claiming between April 2007 and March 2008, you will receive at least £10 if your personal income is lower than £19,513 (or £30,810 if you have a partner or spouse in paid employment). However, these figures will be higher in some circumstances (e.g. if you have a dependant living with you). Also, they may slightly increase from March 2009.

You can still apply if you are working part time and if you are claiming most 'in-work' benefits, such as Adult Education Bursaries,

Working Tax Credit and Child Tax Credit. You will not qualify, however, if you are getting 'out of work' benefits, such as Jobseeker's Allowance. You will not qualify if you are receiving support from other government grants, training allowances or out-of-work benefits. The ALG can be partly ignored for Housing Benefit and Council Tax Benefit purposes. When your local council is working out what Housing Benefit or Council Tax Benefit you are entitled to, it can ignore the first £632 of your ALG payments over a year, but it does not have to. (Note that this figure is valid up to March 2008, but after this date it may increase in line with inflation.) Contact your local council to find out what its policy is.

Free courses

Full-time students aged 16 to 18 who study at a publicly funded school or college do not have to pay tuition fees. If you claim a benefit, or rely on somebody who claims a benefit, you may get your fees paid in full or in part. Some courses are normally free to anyone, and these include Life Skills, such as reading, writing and maths, and English as a Second Language (ESOL).

If you live in the North East or South East of England, you can now get free tuition while you are studying for a level 2 qualification. This pilot scheme is open to anyone over 19 and you can study part time or full time. This new scheme is called Level 2 Entitlement (L2E). Level 2 qualifications are NVQ 2, GCSEs and some vocationally related qualifications, such as Intermediate GNVQ and BTEC First Certificates and Diplomas. There are plans to make the grant available nationally from the 2007/08 academic year. Contact Learn Direct (see *Useful contacts*) for more information.

Educational charities and trusts

Educational charities and trusts may award you funds. They may make small awards towards expenses (such as books and equipment, travel and childcare) which are not covered by other funding sources. You can apply to many educational trusts to piece together the money you need from several small contributions.

Their qualification rules can be anything from where you were born, what your surname is, and what you are studying to how old you are. Apply well in advance, as the process can take time. Be aware of the deadline date for application. Contact EGAS to check which educational trusts you might qualify for.

University or college bursaries

If your tuition fees are over a certain amount (£2,765 in 2007/08) and you receive the full Maintenance Grant or Special Support Grant (which are discussed later in this chapter), your university or college will give you extra financial help. The amounts of bursaries are generally between £300 and £3,000 a year. Rather than pay you in cash, the university or college may provide you with support in kind, such as accommodation, books or help with transport (e.g. a bicycle).

Many institutions are offering more than the minimum amount, and some are offering bursaries to all students. Therefore, it is well worth your contacting the universities or colleges that you are interested in attending to find out exactly what they are offering, or use the search facility on the Universities and Colleges Admissions Service (UCAS) website (see *Useful contacts*).

Many colleges and universities also offer scholarships. These can be based on factors such as your A-level grades, the subjects you studied, or where you live. The scholarships on offer will be different depending on your circumstances and the university or college where you do your course. For example, if you are a member of a trade union or the Labour Party, there is a range of scholarships to apply for if you are able to enrol for a course at Ruskin College (see Chapter 5).

To apply for a bursary or scholarship, you need to approach your university or college directly to find out what is on offer, given your particular circumstances, and about how to apply. The application for bursaries may be handled by your university or college or in some cases by Student Finance Direct (www.studentfinancedirect. co.uk) on its behalf. The main application for student finance asks you to give your consent for Student Finance Direct to share your application details with your university or college, if necessary. Giving your consent allows your university or college to use the information you have provided to assess your entitlement. If you do not consent to this, you will need to provide this information directly to your place of study so that it can carry out its assessment.

Employers

Ask your employer if it will help to pay for your course (see the Introduction, *Test the employer* on page xix). Usually, it will only fund learning related to your job, but some employers will fund a wider range of learning as part of their employee development programmes. Your employers may also give you time off to attend training courses or to prepare coursework.

You should point out the skills you will learn and the benefits to your employer. If it agrees, it may ask you to sign a contract committing you to work for the company for an agreed period.

Some employers will pay your wages and course fees while you study. They tend to be employers who need some research carrying out in a particular field, so this would usually be at postgraduate level. These opportunities are advertised alongside jobs in the usual publications. University careers libraries also stock reference books and information on which companies usually sponsor students.

State financial help for higher education students

General

To qualify for financial help as a higher education student, y meet certain conditions of 'eligibility'. These cover your personal eligibility, your course, and your college or university. Your personal eligibility consists of where you normally live (known as 'residence'), whether you have taken a higher education course before, and your age.

» Your residence

Normally, to qualify for the standard student finance package, on the first day of your course you must:

- » have been 'ordinarily resident' in the UK, Channel Islands or Isle of Man for the three years immediately before starting the course, other than wholly or mainly for the purpose of receiving full-time education;
- » be 'ordinarily resident' in England;
- » have 'settled status' within the UK (under the terms of the Immigration Act 1971).

'Ordinarily resident' means where you normally live and it allows for temporary or occasional times when you are out of the country. 'Settled status' means that there are no immigration restrictions about how long you can stay in the UK. However, you may still qualify for the standard student finance package, even if you do not meet these residence requirements. Ask your local authority or university for advice.

» Previous study

If you have studied before, this may affect your entitlement to student finance. You may not be able to get financial help if you have taken a course of higher education in the past and you either received student finance from the government to do it or the college or university received funding from the government. Generally, you will be entitled to financial help for the length of your course, plus one extra year, if necessary, to cover things such as false starts and transfers. If you are unsure about whether your previous study affects your entitlement to financial help, speak to your local authority or university.

» **Your age**

There are no upper age limits to receive grants or a Student Loan for Fees (see page 146 for more information). However, in order to receive a Student Loan for Maintenance (see page 150), you should be aged under 60 when you start your course. People aged 50 to 54 no longer have to prove that they intend to return to work when they finish their course.

» **Your college or university**

Usually, you can receive student finance if your course takes place at a UK university, a college that receives government funding, a specified private institution (ask your university or college if it qualifies) or a group of schools taking part in the School-Centred Initial Teacher Training (SCITT) scheme.

» **Your course**

Generally, to qualify for finance as a full-time student, your course should lead to a first degree (such as a Bachelor of Arts, Science or Education), a foundation degree, a Diploma of Higher Education (DipHE), a Higher National Diploma (HND), a Higher National Certificate (HNC), an NVQ at level 4 where this is awarded with a first degree, a DipHE or an HND. Part-time courses should last at least one year and should not take more than twice as long as an equivalent full-time course.

Tuition fee loans for higher education students

Universities and colleges in England and Northern Ireland can charge new full-time students up to £3,070 for their courses (2007/08 figure). The amount charged will vary between courses, as well as between different universities and colleges. You can search for information about tuition fees for individual courses through the UCAS website (see *Useful contacts*). Tuition fees at Scottish higher education institutions are set at £1,200 for an HNC or an HND or equivalent; £1,700 for degree or equivalent courses; and £ medicine courses. In Wales, tuition fees are set at £1,200 a

You may be eligible to apply for a tuition fee loan if you are about to take a higher education course, as follows:

» England and Wales

For financial help towards your tuition fees you can apply for a Student Loan for Fees (a tuition fee loan) of up to £3,000 to cover the exact amount of your course fees and the money will be paid directly to your university or college. You will not have to start making repayments until you have left your course and are earning over a certain amount. (Up to March 2008 this is £15,000 a year, but this figure will be higher in some circumstances (e.g. if you have a dependant living with you). Also, it may increase from March 2009.) Your repayments will be nine per cent of your earnings over this set amount. So if, for example, you earned £18,000, your repayments would be £5.19 a week. The interest rate (currently 2.4 per cent) is linked to the rate of inflation, so the amount you repay is the same in real terms as the amount you borrow. If your earnings dropped below £15,000 at any time, your repayments would stop until you were earning over this amount again.

You can apply for student finance online at Student Finance Direct (www.studentfinancedirect.co.uk) or by requesting a paper form that you fill in and send to your local authority. If you normally live in Wales and are studying anywhere in the UK, you can apply for finance through Student Finance Wales. You should apply for any student finance before your course starts, but you can still apply up to nine months after it commences.

To receive a student loan, you must be aged under 60 when you start your course. If you are aged 50 to 54, you no longer have to prove that you intend to return to work when you finish your course.

» Scotland

Scottish residents and EU students who started university or college in Scotland in 2006 will have had their tuition fees paid by the Student Awards Agency for Scotland (SAAS) throughout their study. At the time of writing, most Scottish graduates, however, have to make a payment once they have graduated, but this payment (the Graduate Endowment, which is £2,000 (2007 figure)) is set to be abolished from April 2008. So if you graduated in 2007, it is likely that you will not have to pay it!

If you are normally resident in Scotland but you are studying at an institution outside Scotland, your application for student finance will be dealt with by the SAAS. The amount SAAS pay will depend on your household's income. It could be less than the cost of the tuition fees and if this is the case, then you are expected to pay the difference.

» **Northern Ireland**

Your local Education and Library Board (ELB) will determine what, if any, contribution you have to make towards your fees. For many students their ELB will assist with their course fees. Once you have applied for financial help to your local board, a financial assessment form will be issued. On completing and returning this you will be issued with an SLC Financial Notification detailing your fee and loan entitlements for the coming academic year. Visit the Department of Education (Northern Ireland) website (see *Useful contacts*) if you are not sure where your local ELB is.

If you normally live in Northern Ireland and are studying anywhere in the UK, your application for student finance will be dealt with by Student Finance NI. To find out more, visit the Student Finance NI website at www.studentfinanceni.co.uk.

Part-time study in higher education

» **Fee Grant**

If you are intending to study part time in higher education, you can apply for a Fee Grant to help you with your tuition fees. Your course must last at least one year and it cannot take more than twice as long to complete as an equivalent full-time course. The amount of Fee Grant you can get will depend on your household income (it is income assessed) and on the 'intensity' of your course. 'Intensity' means how long it takes to complete your course compared with an equivalent full-time course. Your college will be able to tell you the intensity of your course. As an example, the intensity of study of a six-year part-time course compared to a three-year full-time course would be 50 per cent, since three is 50 per cent of six. If you already have a degree, you cannot normally apply for this support.

At 2007/08 the maximum Fee Grant for a part-time course with 50 per cent to 59 per cent intensity is £785, for 60 per cent to 74 per cent it is £945, and for 75 per cent or more it is £1,180. You will only receive the full Fee Grant if your household income is £15,700 or lower. If your income is between £15,701 and £23,679, you will only receive a proportion of the grant. You will not receive a grant if your income is £23,680 or more. However, these figures will be higher in some circumstances (e.g. if you have a dependant living with you). Also, the figures may slightly increase from March 2009.

» Course Grant

You can also apply for a Course Grant up to a maximum of £255 for travel, books and other materials (2007/08 figure). For this, the intensity of the course is not relevant, but the above household income figures apply. The grant may slightly increase from March 2009.

To apply for the Fee Grant and Course Grant, you can get an application form (PTG1) from the Department for Children, Schools and Families' information line on 0800 731 9133 or by logging on to www.direct.gov.uk/studentfinance. You should send your applications to your local authority or the Student Loans Company (see *Useful contacts*).

The Open University deals with its own students' applications for the Fee Grant, the Course Grant and the Disabled Students' Allowance (see Chapter 8). It has its own application form it uses instead of the PTG1 – contact the Open University rther details (see *Useful contacts*).

A booklet called *Financial Support for Part-Time Students in Higher Education* sets out the help available in more detail. You can download it from www.direct.gov.uk/studentfinance or you can call the Department for Children, Schools and Families' information line on 0800 731 9133. You may find it harder to find funding to help with your living costs as it is usually assumed that they are met elsewhere (such as through working, savings or benefits).

» **Additional Fee Support Scheme**

If you are studying part time in England only, your university or college may be able to give you extra help towards your tuition fees from the Additional Fee Support Scheme. For example, if your Fee Grant is less than your tuition fees, you may be able to get financial help with some or all of the difference. Your university or college will decide if you can get help and how much help you can get. To find out more, you will need to speak to the student department at your college that runs the Access to Learning Fund (see below), as it will also be responsible for the Additional Fee Support Scheme.

Access to Learning Fund

If you are a full-time or part-time higher education student in England, or you are doing a postgraduate course, there is a special hardship fund called the Access to Learning Fund, which you can obtain from your university or college. It will look at your individual circumstances and you may be able to get help for course or living costs that are not already covered by other grants (e.g. everyday living costs, childcare costs or support over the summer holiday if you have no one else to turn to). The university or college may also consider emergency payments to cover unexpected financial crises or exceptional costs, such as repairs to household equipment. It is likely that it will give you priority if you are thinking of giving up your course because of financial difficulties and you need financial help to keep studying, or if you are from a low-income family, are disabled or you are a parent with your children living with you.

You normally apply through the student services department at your university or college. It will tell you exactly what information you need to supply, but you should be ready to provide a copy of the letter from Student Finance Direct showing how much you will get through the standard student finance package, together with documents showing your financial situation, such as bank statements and details of your rent. Usually, you apply after you start your course. By this time you will know how much you are getting through the standard student finance package. But if you know you are going to need extra help, it is a good idea to approach your university or college before your course starts.

Student Loan for Maintenance for higher education students (living cost loan)

You can take out a Student Loan for Maintenance (a living cost loan) to help pay your living costs during term times and holidays. The total amount you can borrow will depend on factors such as your household income, where you live while you are studying and how much Maintenance Grant you receive. You can apply for around 75 per cent of the Student Loan for Maintenance regardless of your household income ('non-income assessed'). Whether you can apply for the remainder will depend upon your household income ('income assessed'). If you receive the Special Support Grant, this has no effect on the amount of Student Loan for Maintenance you can borrow.

Although this loan is separate from the tuition fee loans (see page 145), you can apply for both of them on a single form, through the same company. The same repayment rules apply as for Student Loan for Fees. You get a smaller loan in your final year, as it only has to cover you until the end of the final term.

For students in Scotland, there is an income-assessed loan of up to £575 available for some young students from families with an income of £17,400 or less, which goes down to zero for a family with an income over £20,695. (These 2007 figures may increase slightly in line with inflation from March 2008.) You may also be eligible to claim for non-repayable supplementary grants, such as travelling expenses. These are dependent on your own and your parents' income. For further information, visit the SAAS website (see *Useful contacts*).

Maintenance Grant

In England and Wales you may be eligible for a yearly Maintenance Grant of up to £2,835. This grant is non-repayable. How much you receive depends on your household income and the year of study. For example, you will receive the full grant if your household income is less than £18,360 and you will receive a partial grant if your household income is between £18,360 and £39,304. However, these figures will be higher in some circumstances (e.g. if you have a dependant living with you). Also, these 2007/08 figures may slightly increase from March 2009. If you are from Northern Ireland, the amount of the grant is currently up to a maximum of £3,265.

If you are getting a higher level of Maintenance Grant, it is assumed that you will not need to borrow as much through the Student Loan for Maintenance. To reflect this, some of the Maintenance Grant is paid instead of the Student Loan for Maintenance. If you get £1,260 or more of the Maintenance Grant, the amount you can borrow through your loan will be reduced by £1,260.

In Scotland, if you are aged 24 or under and are living and studying in Scotland for a full-time higher education course, you may be able to apply for a 'young student bursary'. This is non-repayable and it can replace part of the student loan. It is administered by the SAAS. You have to be unmarried and not self-supporting through earnings or benefits for at least three years previously. The amount of the bursary depends on your family income. The maximum award is £2,510, whether you are living at home or not. No bursary is payable to anyone with a family income over £32,515.

The Students' Outside Scotland Bursary (SOSB) is available to Scottish students studying a higher education course full time at UK institutions outside of Scotland. This is paid instead of part of the loan, reducing the amount students need to take out. The highest amount available is £2,000 for those students whose family income is below £17,940. (Note that these 2007 figures will be higher in some circumstances (e.g. if you have a dependant living with you) and they may increase slightly in line with inflation from March 2008.)

Currently the bursary is not available for those students whose family income is above £32,515 (2007 figure).

For further information, visit the SAAS website (see *Useful contacts*).

Special Support Grant (SSG)

In England or Wales, if you are a full-time student who is eligible for income-related welfare benefits (such as Income Support and Housing Benefit), while you are studying you may be able to get an SSG, which is a non-repayable grant, currently up to £2,835. This grant may apply to you if you are a lone parent, one of a student couple with children, or a disabled person. If you are from Northern Ireland, the SSG is currently up to £3,265 a year for new full-time students.

The SSG will not affect the amount of welfare benefits or tax credits you are entitled to. If you receive this grant, you will not be eligible for the Maintenance Grant, but it will have no effect on the amount of Student Loan for Maintenance you can borrow.

Again, these 2007 figures will be higher in some circumstances (e.g. if you have a dependant living with you) and they may increase slightly in line with inflation from March 2008.

Financial support for City & Guilds students

If you are going to study for a course that leads to a City & Guilds qualification, you can apply for an access bursary (educational grant). City & Guilds can offer financial assistance to a small number of people who are finding it difficult to pay the bills while they study for a City & Guilds qualification. It may be able to help you with paying course fees (if no other funding is available), covering the cost of a break from work while you study, paying childcare or travel costs, or helping towards the cost of essential equipment or materials.

Only applicants aged 16 or over who are currently living in the UK and intend to enrol on a City & Guilds course within the UK can be considered. Log on to the City & Guilds website (see *Useful contacts*) to download an application form.

You can submit your application at any time. Applications are considered twice a year (in June and December) and you will be notified soon after that whether you have been chosen to go forward to the next stage (an interview). If you miss one cut-off date, your application will automatically go into the next application period.

Learner Support Funds

You can apply for Learner Support Funds if you are 16 or over and finding it hard to make ends meet when you are at college or sixth form college. Learner Support Funds were previously known as 'Access Funds' and they can be used for financial hardship and emergencies, childcare costs (Ofsted registered), accommodation costs (for those who have to study beyond daily travelling distance), tuition, registration and exam fees, travel costs (including university interview travel costs), essential course-related equipment and materials, and field trips.

Schools and colleges set their own criteria and manage their own procedures. This means that the amount of funds available to individuals and the way funds are allocated may differ. Some funds, including childcare and residential funds, have maximum amounts available. Common priority groups are the economically disadvantaged (such as those on benefit or a low income); students who are disabled, mentally ill or have learning difficulties; those aged over 19 who do not have a level 2 qualification; and students who have been in care, on probation, young parents, or others considered 'at risk'.

If you qualify, payment could be in cash to you or via a third party, or it could pay for goods and services. Your payment could be a loan, which you have to pay back, or a grant, which you do not have to repay.

You cannot claim if you are receiving full student finance for higher education, or if you are on a Learn Direct course or on most New Deal programmes, or if you are training while you are in work (e.g. as an apprentice). There is a New Deal exception, though, which is the New Deal for Lone Parents.

If you are at college, you can apply through the Student Support or Welfare Officer. If you are in sixth form, you can apply through the Student Awards or Student Support Officer at your LEA. You may be expected to provide proof of income or expenditure when you apply.

Grants specific to Wales

» Assembly Learning Grant

This is a means-tested award for students from lower income families and it can be up to £1,500 a year (up to March 2008, but it may increase slightly after this date). You do not have to pay it back. You apply for it from your LEA.

» Individual Learning Accounts (ILAs)

To qualify, you must be aged 18 or over and be living in Wales. Also, you or your partner must be claiming Income Support, Jobseeker's Allowance (income based), Pension Credit, Housing Benefit, Working Tax Credit or Council Tax Benefit. However, you can still claim if you are not on any of these benefits if you have no qualifications above level 2 in the NQF; that is, nothing higher than GCSE (grade A to G, GNVQ intermediate level, NVQ level 1 or 2, GNVQ foundation level or a BTEC First Certificate). For more information, visit the ILA Wales site at www.ilawales.co.uk.

» **Passport to Study Grant**

Some LEAs award these to 16–19 year-olds who stay on in full-time education. It is for expenses such as books, travel and equipment.

Further information on funding in Wales is available from Learning Wales at www.learning.wales.gov.uk/students.

Grants specific to Scotland

» **Further Education Bursaries**

These are awarded by colleges throughout Scotland. Whether you qualify depends on your personal circumstances and the course you intend to study. You can contact the college you plan to attend to discuss your student support package. For more details, call Learn Direct Scotland or visit the website of the Scottish Executive (see *Useful contacts* for details).

» **Individual Learning Accounts (ILAs)**

ILA Scotland can help you pay for a wide range of learning. It is mainly aimed at people on lower incomes or on benefits. For information on the scheme, visit the ILA Scotland website or phone the ILA Scotland helpline (see *Useful contacts*) for advice on what learning is available.

Grants specific to Northern Ireland

» **College Support Fund**

This means-tested award is for students who get into financial difficulties when they are on a course. It covers course-related expenses, such as travel, books, childcare and equipment. Each college has its own rules on who qualifies. Ask the Student Support or Welfare office at your college for details.

» **Additional Support Fund**

This is for students with disabilities to help them meet

additional costs, such as specialist equipment. Colleges have their own rules for who qualifies. Ask your Student Support or Welfare office at your college for details.

» **Education Library Board (ELB) Discretionary Award**

The ELB awards some students with additional help towards course-related costs, such as travel. Rules of qualification vary from region to region. Check your region for more information.

Further information on the funding system in Northern Ireland is available from the Department for Employment and Learning (Northern Ireland) (see *Useful contacts*).

Welfare benefits while you study

You may be eligible for certain welfare benefits if your income drops because you reduce your hours of employment or stop working altogether to study. If you are on benefits, you may be able to continue receiving them in some cases, but this is not always the case. You may still be eligible if you are disabled, with dependants, or you are a lone parent, both while you are studying and during the long summer holiday. The rules will be different depending on your personal circumstances, and whether you are studying part time or full time.

Usually, if you are attending a course or studying from home or at work, there should be no effect on welfare benefits. Below is a guide, but take advice from the body that pays you the benefits, or the CAB, or other advice service for more information.

Child Tax Credit

If you are attending a course full time: Students with dependent children may be entitled, regardless of whether they are working and subject to Income Tax.

If you are attending a course part time: No effect.

Working Tax Credit

If you are attending a course full time: As a student, you need to have a child or a disability and be working over 16 hours a week in addition to studying, or if you manage to work over 30 hours a week, then you can claim without having a child or a disability.

Working Tax Credit has a childcare element where you can get back up to 70 per cent of your costs for qualifying childcare. A student, or his spouse or partner, cannot receive a Childcare Grant from his local authority if he receives the childcare element of the Working Tax Credit from HM Revenue & Customs (HMRC). You can decide which one you want to claim.

If you are attending a course part time: No effect.

Council Tax Benefit

If you are attending a course full time: If you live in an all-student household, you should not be liable for Council Tax anyway. Ask at your college or university for proof of your full-time student status which you can present to your local authority.

If you do not live in an all-student household, you will be able to stay on Council Tax Benefit as a full-time student if you also receive Income Support or Jobseeker's Allowance, or you are a lone parent, or a student couple with one or more children, or you are disabled.

If you are attending a course part time: You may be liable to pay Council Tax, but you should be able to claim Council Tax Benefit as normal if you are eligible.

Income Support if you are in non-advanced education

If you are attending a course full time: If you are a young person aged 18 to 24 and you are attending an unwaged Work Based Learning Programme in England or a Skillseekers course (in Scotland), you may be able to get Income Support.

If you are a full-time student aged 16 to 19 and you are in 'non-advanced education' (i.e. anything up to and including GCE A-level), and one of these circumstances apply:

» You are so severely disabled that you are unlikely to get a job in the next 12 months.

» You are an orphan, and you have no one who is acting for you as a parent.

» You would be in danger if you lived with your parents (or any person acting in their place). This could, for example, be a situation where you might be in physical danger or where the stress might cause you harm.

» Your relationship with your parents is so poor that you cannot live with them (this is usually referred to as 'estrangement').

» You live apart from your parents as they are unable to support you as they are chronically sick or disabled, or they are barred from entering the country as immigrants, or they are in prison.

If you are attending a course part time: No effect.

Income Support if you are in advanced education

If you are attending a course full time: If you are a full-time student in 'advanced education' (i.e. beyond A-level), you can receive your Income Support in term time, as well as during holidays, if:

» You are a single parent living with your child who is under the age of 16 (a foster child will count).

» You are a student from another country outside the UK and you are temporarily without funds.

» You are disabled or ill and you qualify for the disability premium or severe disability premium, or you have been too ill to work for the past 28 weeks.

» You are deaf and qualify for Disabled Students Allowance.

If you are claiming as a couple and you are both full-time students and either one of you or both of you are responsible for a child (for which you receive Child Benefit), you can still claim, but only in the summer holiday.

If you are attending a course part time: No effect.

Pension Credit

If you are attending a course full time: No effect.

If you are attending a course part time: No effect.

Disability Living Allowance

If you are attending a course full time: No effect.

If you are attending a course part time: No effect.

Housing Benefit

If you are attending a course full time: Most full-time students are not entitled to claim Housing Benefit during the whole of their course, including the summer holiday.

Full-time students who can claim Housing Benefit:

» Lone parents.

» Those who are getting Income Support or Jobseeker's Allowance (income based) will automatically be entitled to claim Housing Benefit.

» Disabled people and those who have been awarded a Disabled Student's Allowance due to deafness.

» Those who are under 20 and are following a course of further education (but not higher education), unless they live at home with their parents.

» Those who live with a partner who is also a student and they have dependent children.

» Those who are solely responsible for a child boarded out with them by a local council or voluntary organisation.

» Those whose study has been interrupted due to illness or

> caring responsibilities, who are not allowed to rejoin their course until a later date and are not eligible for a student loan for this period.
>
> » Pensioners.
>
> » Those who are on Work Based Learning for Adults and getting a training allowance from the Department for Work and Pensions, and who are not classed as a student for Housing Benefit purposes.
>
> If you are entitled to claim Housing Benefit, you can continue to claim it in the summer holiday. Although, if you are claiming Housing Benefit for accommodation just so you can be near your college, you cannot get Housing Benefit for any week that you are away.
>
> If you are in a hall of residence or other accommodation rented from your educational establishment, you will not be able to claim Housing Benefit during your period of study. The only exception is where your college does not own the accommodation but rents it for your use. (This is not the case if your college rents your accommodation from another educational establishment. Colleges are not allowed to let others manage their accommodation just to enable students to claim Housing Benefit.)
>
> If you pay rent to someone who you live with and he is a close relative or your tenancy or rental agreement is not on a commercial basis , you will not be entitled to Housing Benefit.
>
> In any other accommodation you can claim Housing Benefit, even during your period of study.
>
> **If you are attending a course part time:** No effect.

> ## Jobseeker's Allowance
>
> **If you are attending a course full time:** Eligible students must meet the 'labour market conditions' of being available and actively seeking work. So the times when you can claim Jobseeker's Allowance are limited, but they include:

» If you are one of a couple who are both full-time students and responsible for at least one child, you may apply during the summer holiday. However, the person who claims will have to be available for and actively seek full-time work. If you are a full-time student but your partner is not, then he can claim Jobseeker's Allowance throughout the year (but if your partner qualifies for Income Support in his own right, he may claim that instead).

» If you are aged 25 or over and have been unemployed for two years or more, you may be able to do a full-time employment-related course for up to a year and still get Jobseeker's Allowance.

» If you were absent from your course intermittingly due to illness or caring responsibilities, you can claim from when the reason for your absence has ceased until the day before you rejoin your course or the start of the next academic year, whichever is the earlier.

If you are attending a course part time: You may qualify for Jobseeker's Allowance, but you will have to fill in a 'Jobseeker's Agreement', which will require that you state that you will give up your course if you are offered full-time work, or alternatively rearrange your hours to suit work.

You must be willing to go to a job interview, even if you have to take time off from your course. You should also be prepared to rearrange your hours of study to fit around a job.

Incapacity Benefit

If you are attending a course full time: If you already claim Incapacity Benefit, you may be able to carry on receiving it as a student.

The Disability Officer or Student Services Officer at you' college or university will be able to advise you. You c₂ information from the National Bureau for Students ' Disabilities (Skill) (see *Useful contacts* for details).

If you are attending a course part time: No ef'

Paying for childcare while you study

Free childcare places

A child aged four is eligible for a free part-time place. In some areas this is available to children aged three. Places can be in a school nursery or reception classes, day nurseries, playgroups or with some childminders. Contact your local Children's Information Service (CIS) for more details. ChildcareLink can put you in touch with your local CIS. Call the organisation on 0800 096 0296 or visit the ChildcareLink website at www.childcarelink.gov.uk.

Care to Learn

Young parents in England going back into learning can now get financial help with childcare. You can apply for Care to Learn funding if you start a course of learning or training in a school, college or as a trainee with a work-based learning provider that receives some public funding. As long as you begin the course before you are 20, Care to Learn will contribute towards your childcare costs until the course has finished. You can claim Care to Learn either as the child's father or mother, as long as:

» the other parent is unable to provide childcare (because, for example, he is working);

» the other parent is not claiming Childcare Tax Credit.

If you have more than one child, you can get help for each of them. You have to use a registered childcare provider.

For more information and application forms, log on to the government's website at www.dfes.gov.uk/caretolearn or contact the Care to Learn team on 0845 600 2809.

Childcare Grant

are a full-time student with dependent children under 15 (or

17 if your child is registered as having special educational needs), the amount you receive will depend on your actual childcare costs and on your income and that of your dependants. You must use a registered childcare provider or carer approved under the new Childcare Approval Scheme. A Childcare Grant cannot be paid for any period when the child is entitled to free, early year education provision, although it may be used to pay for services before and/or after that provision.

If your childcare arrangements meet these requirements, you will be able to get 85 per cent of the cost of childcare throughout the whole year, currently up to a limit of £148.75 a week (85 per cent of the actual costs up to £175 a week) for one child and up to £255 per week for two or more. These figures are up to March 2008, and they may increase slightly after this date. The grant is paid in three instalments with your student loan. Jobcentre Plus will not count any help you receive when working out your benefit entitlement. It is government policy that you cannot get a Childcare Grant if you are claiming the childcare element of the Working Tax Credit.

To apply for the Childcare Grant, you will need to tell your local authority at the time you apply for other financial support. It will send you a form, *Application for help with childcare costs* (CCG1). You should complete section 1 of the form and ask your childcare provider to fill in section 2.

A second form, *Confirmation of Childcare Payments* (CCG2), asks for evidence of childcare payments made to your childcare provider and for any change of circumstances. You should fill in part 1 of the form and ask your provider to fill in and sign sections 2 and 3 before sending it to your local authority. If you return the form after the dates shown on the form, your next instalment of Childcare Grant may not be paid. You can also download the CCG1 and CCG2 forms at the Student Finance Direct's website at www.studentfinancedirect. co.uk.

For information about childcare in your area, visit the ChildcareLink website at www.childcarelink.gov.uk.

Parents' Learning Allowance (PLA)

If you are a full-time student with a dependent child or children, you may be eligible for a PLA grant to cover childcare expenses, travel costs, books and equipment, and your extra costs if you have to run two homes as a result of living away. It is paid on top of any standard student finance you may receive. You do not have to repay it. You can apply if you receive the Childcare Grant. The allowance is also available to students with low incomes.

The amount of PLA you can get will depend on your income and your dependants' income. The maximum you can get is £1,400 a year up to March 2008. This figure may slightly increase after this date. You apply for this grant through your local authority. It is paid in three instalments from the Student Loans Company with your loan. Jobcentre Plus should not count this grant when they work out your benefit entitlement.

The grants are managed by your LEA or in Scotland, the SAAS. Ask the authority for details of its claims procedures and priorities for help. The SAAS or the Department for Children, Schools and Families' information line can provide further advice, as can the National Union of Students – see *Useful contacts.*

Paying for adult dependants' care while you study

Adult Dependants' Grant

If you have a spouse or partner, or you have another member of your family who is financially dependent on you, you may be eligible for the Adult Dependants' Grant. How much you get depends on your income and that of your dependants, and the maximum is £2,455 a year up to March 2008 (this figure may slightly increase after this date). To apply for the Adult Dependants' Grant, you will need to tell your local authority at the time you apply for other financial support.

The grant is paid in three instalments with your student loan and it will be counted as income in any Jobcentre Plus or HMRC assessments.

Postgraduate funding

General

Postgraduate funding is different from funding for further and higher education because very little of it is automatic. Most postgraduate students have to hunt around to find the money they need. There is also competition for funding, as funds are limited. So plan well in advance, and sort out your funding at least a year before your course starts.

Career Development Loans (see page 138) and the Disabled Students' Allowance (see Chapter 8) should be available for postgraduate study. Otherwise, you may be able to apply for a Discretionary Award from your LEA, depending on its policy. Some universities offer paid research posts that give you the opportunity to also study a postgraduate course. Some postgraduate students also lecture part-time to fund further study.

In Scotland there is the Postgraduate Students' Allowances Scheme. Under this scheme you can apply for financial help with some vocational postgraduate courses. Another possibility is the Scottish Studentship Scheme where you might be able to get help for a full-time postgraduate course. Contact the university you are applying to for more details.

Research councils

Depending on which subject you study, you might be able to get funding from a research council. Funding is usually awarded for research rather than taught courses, but competition is keen. You do not apply directly to the council; instead you apply through the university.

The research councils are:

» The Engineering and Physical Sciences Research Council

» The Natural Environment Research Council

» The Particle Physics and Astronomy Research Council

» The Arts and Humanities Research Board

» The Medical Research Council

» The Bio-technology and Biological Science Research Council

» The Economic and Social Research Council

» The Council for the Central Laboratory of the Research Councils

Finance to study specific subjects

There are a number of funding sources for specific occupations. Some of them are listed here, but for further information log on to the Prospects Postgraduate Funding Guide at www.prospects.ac.uk.

» **Law**

It is possible to qualify for a Discretionary Award for the different stages of a law course. This depends on the funding policy of your LEA. Contact your local LEA for more details. Some students also find bursaries from law firms or the Law Society (www.lawsociety.org.uk). Loans may also be available from law schools.

» **Social work**

In England, Scotland and Wales you may qualify for a bursary for a full-time postgraduate diploma in social work. Log on to the General Social Care Council or Social Work Careers websites for more information (see *Useful contacts*). A bursary system also exists in Northern Ireland. Visit the Northern Ireland Social Care Council for information (see *Useful contacts*).

» Dance and drama

If you have potential, you may be able to get a Dance and Drama Award to cover your costs. To be eligible, dance students have to be aged 16 or over and drama students have to be 18 or over. The awards are available from some of England's leading private dance and drama schools and they can help you pay for a place on a prestigious and well-respected course. The awards are means-tested and intended to help students from low-income families be trained in performing arts. There are more places than awards, so you may not automatically qualify for an award. The award will pay for the majority of your tuition fees, but you will also be expected to make a contribution. You could also get extra money to help with your living costs.

» NHS Bursary

An NHS Bursary is a lump sum from the NHS that you do not have to pay back. It can cover living costs and some additional expenses if you are studying to work for the NHS. It can help towards tuition fees, travel and housing costs, and it provides help for students with dependants, older students, single parents, and students with disabilities.

There are two types of NHS Bursary: means-tested and non-means-tested. How much you get on a means-tested bursary depends on your circumstances (your income, partner's income or parents' income).

Non-means-tested bursaries are set at a flat rate, and they do not depend on your circumstances. Which one you will qualify for depends on which type of health course you are doing.

Means-tested NHS bursaries are for:

» allied health profession courses (occupational therapy, chiropody, dietetics, orthoptics, physiotherapy, prosthetics and orthotics, speech and language therapy, radiography, and recognised audiology/hearing therapy courses);

» dental auxiliary courses (dental hygiene and dental therapy);

» nursing and midwifery degree courses (not the diploma courses, which are covered by non-means-tested bursaries).

Non means-tested bursaries are for:

» diploma courses that lead to registration as a nurse or midwife;

» operating department practitioner (ODP) courses.

There are some differences for students in Scotland, Wales and Northern Ireland. You can view more information on NHS Bursaries on the Department of Health website (see *Useful contacts*). More information is also available from:

» NHS England (tel: 0845 358 6655)

» NHS Wales (tel: 029 2026 1495)

» NHS Scotland (tel: 0131 476 8212)

» NHS Northern Ireland (tel: 028 9025 7777)

» Teaching

You have to pay tuition fees if you are studying for a Postgraduate Certificate in Education (PGCE) or School Centred Initial Teaching Training (SCITT). However, you can apply for a tuition fee loan to pay the fees (see page 145). Tuition fees are different in Wales, so the support arrangements are also different. If you study an undergraduate degree (usually a Bachelor of Education (BEd)) leading to Qualified Teacher Status (QTS), you do not get any special help; you can apply for the same funding support as other students on undergraduate courses. If you are enrolled on a postgraduate route to QTS, you may be eligible to receive a training bursary ranging from £6,000 to £9,000 (these 2007 figures may slightly increase after March 2008), depending on the subject you are training to teach. Students in England are also eligible for a non-means-tested grant of £1,200 and be able to apply for an additional means-tested grant of £1,500. Again, these 2007 figures may slightly increase after March 2008. You may also qualify for a bursary. How much you get depends on the subject you want to train in, and where and when you train. You get more if you apply to teach shortage subjects such as maths, science, modern languages and music. You may also be eligible for a golden hello of several thousand pounds if you train to teach a shortage subject. Log on to the Student Finance section of www.direct.gov.uk or the Training and Development Agency for Schools (see *Useful contacts*) for full details of support available for PGCE students.

Chapter 8

If you are disabled

New Deal for Disabled People

If you receive welfare benefits because you are disabled or suffer from ill health, the New Deal for Disabled People (NDDP) may help you develop new skills and improve your confidence, and ultimately help you into paid employment. Unlike some New Deal schemes, this one is not compulsory. The programme is delivered through a network of 'job brokers' from a range of organisations. Each job broker offers different services which can be tailored to your individual needs.

Your job broker will talk to you about your situation and the sort of work you are looking for. You will be helped in deciding on your best route into employment, and the broker will work with you to achieve your goals. He will assist you with job hunting, job applications and interview forms. He will identify your training needs, if you have any, and then work with local training providers to get the training you need. The broker may also be able to help you with travel costs to interviews or even pay for some of your costs while you are looking for work. He has to understand any barriers to employment you may face (e.g. lack of skills or confidence, or the fear of having welfare benefits altered or reduced) and he will aim to help you overcome these problems.

The job broker also works closely with the employers to help make sure that things work out for you in your job, including helping you to apply for help from the Access to Work Scheme. This scheme gives you extra support in the workplace (e.g. special adaptations or equipment, or a support worker). The job broker will help you apply for help with this, but do note that you do not have to be eligible for the New Deal to benefit from the scheme. All employees with any disability are eligible.

You can join the NDDP programme if you receive one or more of the following benefits:

» Incapacity Benefit.

» Income Support including a disability premium.

» Income Support because your Incapacity Benefit has been stopped and you are appealing against the decision.

» National Insurance credits because of incapacity (you may get these on their own or with Income Support, Housing Benefit, Council Tax Benefit or War Pension).

» Disability Living Allowance, provided that you do not get Jobseeker's Allowance and are not in paid work for 16 hours or more a week.

» Housing Benefit with a disability premium, provided that you are not getting Jobseeker's Allowance and are not in paid work for 16 hours or more a week.

» Council Tax Benefit, provided that you do not get Jobseeker's Allowance and are not in paid work for 16 hours or more a week.

» War Pension with an Unemployability Supplement.

» Industrial Injuries Disablement Benefit with an Unemployability Supplement.

» A benefit equivalent to Incapacity Benefit from a European Union (EU) member country.

For more information, log on to the Jobcentre Plus website at www.jobcentreplus.gov.uk or call the NDDP helpline on 0800 137 177 (textphone 0800 435 550). You can also locate your local job broker on the job broker search website at www.jobbrokersearch. co.uk. When you register with the job broker he will ask you for brief information about yourself and he will arrange an appointment with you so he can begin helping you.

College and university education

Universities and colleges should do the best they can to accommodate your needs if you are disabled. When you are considering whether to apply, contact them in advance to establish how they can meet your needs, then follow this up with a visit, either on an open day or evening or separate appointment. Ask for their 'disability statement' – most colleges and universities produce them – and it will give you more background information as to what the university can offer you. You could also consider talking to college advisers, union welfare officers or the student union disability officers.

University and college education is now covered by Part 4 of the Disability Discrimination Act (DDA). By law, institutions are required to make 'reasonable' adjustments to ensure that disabled students are not placed at a 'substantial disadvantage'. This means that universities and colleges must not discriminate against disabled students in enrolment and admissions, in the provision of student services and in exclusions. This includes the provision of auxiliary aids and services, and adjustments to the physical environment. For more information about education and the DDA, contact Skill (the National Bureau for Students with Disabilities) – see *Useful contacts* for details.

HELP AND ADVICE

There are a number of websites you can visit for help and advice about learning with a disability:

» Connexions (see *Useful contacts*), if you are under 19.

» Learn Direct (see *Useful contacts*), if you are over 19.

» Skill (see *Useful contacts*) is a national charity promoting opportunities for young people and adults with any kind of disability in post-16 education, training and employment across the UK.

» The website of the Royal National Institute of Blind People (RNIB) offers information, support and advice to over two million people with sight problems. See *Useful contacts* for details.

» The website www.direct.gov.uk has a lot of information about the types of financial help that is available for students with disabilities. Visit www.direct.gov.uk/en/ DisabledPeople/EducationAndTraining/index.htm.

» Student Finance Direct is the main government site to help you find out more about financial support in higher education. The site includes online applications. Log on to www.studentfinancedirect.co.uk.

» There is also a website written by a boy who has dyslexia. The site contains lots of useful information including tips for people with dyslexia, a question and answer section and success stories of people who have overcome their disability. Visit the site at www.iamdyslexic.com.

» After 16 is a website which is aimed at teenagers and young people in the UK who have an impairment or disability and are wondering what opportunities and services are out there when they leave school. Find out more at www.after16.org.uk.

Disabled Students' Allowance

A Disabled Students' Allowance is a grant to help you meet the extra costs of studying which you may incur as a direct result of a disability or specific learning difficulty. It is designed to help disabled students study on an equal basis with other students.

The allowances are paid on top of the standard student finance package. The amount you can get does not depend on your household income and the allowance does not have to be repaid.

The Disabled Students' Allowance covers four types of help:

1. Specialist equipment you need for studying (e.g. computer software).

2. A non-medical helper, such as a note-taker or reader.

3. Extra travel costs you have to pay because of your disability.

4. Other costs (e.g. tapes or Braille paper).

Student Finance Direct will pay the money into your account as needed, or directly to the supplier of services (e.g. your university, college or equipment supplier).

To qualify for a Disabled Students' Allowance, you will need to meet the conditions for eligibility set out under *State financial help for higher education students* in Chapter 7. To apply, you will then have to show your local authority (or the Open University) written proof of your disability from an appropriate medical professional. If you have a specific learning difficulty, such as dyslexia or dyspraxia, the local authority may ask you to have an independent assessment carried out to establish this. Your local authority cannot meet the costs of this assessment. If you cannot afford to pay for it, you can apply to your college or university for help through the Learner Support Fund (see Chapter 7).

You can apply if you are studying:

» a full-time course that lasts at least one year (including a distance learning course);

» a part-time course that lasts one year and does not take more than twice as long to complete as an equivalent full-time course (including an Open University or other distance learning course).

You will not be eligible for a Disabled Students' Allowance if you receive a bursary from the National Health Service (NHS). If you are a postgraduate student, you will not qualify if you receive a bursary or award from a research council, the General Social Care Council, your college or university (if the support is equivalent to Disabled

Students' Allowances) or the NHS. Also, you will not be eligible to apply if you are an EU or other international student.

How much you will get will depend on your particular circumstances. If you are a part-time student, the intensity of your course will also affect how much you can receive. As a guide, in 2007/08 the maximum you can claim for specialist equipment is £4,905 for the entire course, for a non-medical helper you can get £12,420 a year (£9,315 a year for a part-time course) and General Disabled Students' Allowances are £1,640 a year for a full-time course and £1,230 a year for a part-time course. You can also claim 'reasonable spending' on extra travel costs. Postgraduate students (including distance learners and relevant Open University students) can apply for a single allowance to cover all of their costs. The maximum amount is £5,915 for the year. The allowances will not count when the local authority is working out your entitlement to benefits or tax credits.

If your disability becomes more severe during your course, you can apply to have another assessment to identify any further help you may need. If you want to transfer to another course, you will still be entitled to receive Disabled Students' Allowances. However, if you need different equipment and have already used up your maximum equipment allowance, you will not be able to receive any more. If you have not used the maximum, the remainder will be available to you.

HELP AND ADVICE

You can get more information about Disabled Students' Allowances from the Department for Children, Schools and Families' booklet *Bridging the Gap*. This can be downloaded from the Student Finance Direct website or you can get it from your local education authority (LEA).

If you are a full-time student, you can apply for Disabled Students' Allowance at the same time as you apply for student finance from your LEA (see Chapter 7). Tick the box on the main application and follow any other instructions on the form. You may be sent another form to complete.

If you are studying part time or doing a postgraduate course, you need to get application form DSA1 from your LEA or download it from the Student Finance Direct site and take it to your college or university. Ask the college to sign it and then send it to the address printed on the form. If you are a part-time higher education student, you will not need to get the form signed if the college has already completed its section of the PTG1 form (the part-time student form).

If you are an Open University student, you should apply directly to the Open University's Disabled Students' Allowances (DSA) office. If you tell the Open University that you have a disability when you apply, the office will send you the application form automatically.

Chapter 9

Choosing an occupation

If you are looking to find a new job, there are numerous occupations to choose from. Space does not permit me to detail all of them individually, so below is a list of the different types of occupations which have been grouped into sectors to help you get started on your quest. Sample salaries are also given.

When you have an idea of the type of occupation you are looking for, you may want to carry out more research. You can use the following methods to do so:

» **Search online**

Use the internet or try your local library. Reference books and websites often explain about qualifications and provide details of useful associations and websites which may help you to obtain relevant work experience or a career opportunity.

» **Prospects**

You could also try the Prospects website (www.prospects.ac.uk), although it is mostly geared to graduates.

» **Trade magazines**

Buying a subscription to one of the trade magazines is also an excellent way to learn about the current issues within the industry and to find out about courses or jobs. You c͟ ͟ ͟ ͟ go to a trade or recruitment fair.

» Connexions

Log on to the Connexions Occupations 4u site at www.connexions-direct.com/jobs4u for a comprehensive list of occupations, the skills required for each, the entry qualifications, and the rates of pay and prospects.

» Learn Direct

At www.learndirect-advice.co.uk/helpwithyourcareer/jobprofiles/ you can browse through over 700 job profiles by choosing a category using the search facility. Learn Direct publishes a series of booklets covering many work sectors, subjects and careers. Each book contains case studies showing people in a variety of jobs. They tell you how it is, including the good things and the bad. Each job shows you what qualifications you need, what training you can get, and how much you may be paid.

» The Sector Skills Council

Contact a Sector Skills Council (SSC) relevant to the occupation you have in mind to find out about training and career opportunities. The different SSCs are listed throughout this chapter and all their contact details can be found in *Useful contacts* at the back of this book.

There are 25 SSCs and their four key goals are to reduce skills gaps and shortages; to improve productivity, business and public service performance; to increase opportunities to boost the skills and productivity of everyone in the sector's workforce; and to improve learning supply including apprenticeships, higher education and National Occupational Standards (NOS).

Together, the SSCs cover approximately 89 per cent of the UK workforce. The Sector Skills Development Agency (SSDA) has responsibility for providing cover for those industries that fall outside the SSCs and it actively engages with trade unions and professional bodies in this role. Visit its site for further information, where there is a link to the individual SSC for each sector. See *Useful contacts* for details.

Prospects for development

When it comes to prospects, in general occupations in all sectors provide opportunities for development. In many cases apprenticeships and opportunities for Continuing Professional Development (CPD) (see the Introduction) will be available, or training for new qualifications, to help you climb the career ladder or to achieve specialist or professional status.

However, when you are considering applying for a job with an individual employer in the sector you are advised to find out more about its policies and culture to see what opportunities it makes available, if any. (For more information, see the Introduction, *Test the employer* on page xix.)

Administration and management

The occupations

Every organisation, large or small, needs effective administration. People working in this sector provide the support the organisation needs to meet its objectives.

Roles in this job family range from managers, who devise policies and make decisions, to clerical workers, who collect, store, interpret and distribute information. Occupations may involve supervising colleagues or dealing with clients, members of the public and representatives of other organisations, either face to face or on the telephone.

There are opportunities in every employment sector, including national government (the civil service) and local government, agriculture, engineering, finance, health, leisure, media, retail, transport and utilities. The Civil Service Fast Stream is designed to develop graduates rapidly and equip them to work in the senior civil service. Fast streamers work in a range of roles in their employing departments.

Skill check

Here are the main skills required:

» Good people and communication skills.

» The ability to work well in a team.

» In many cases a commitment to providing a high quality of customer care and an enjoyment of dealing with the public.

» Good literacy and numeracy skills.

» Basic computer skills including the use of office software applications, such as Word.

» The ability to problem solve and use initiative.

» Good organisational skills and a methodical approach.

» The ability to work under pressure and meet deadlines.

» The ability to research and analyse information.

» Supervisors and managers also need leadership and decision-making skills.

» For some roles, specialist qualifications in languages or knowledge of medical or legal terminology may be essential.

ENTRY QUALIFICATIONS

Requirements vary depending on the employer and the skills required of the particular job it is recruiting for. Some vacancies are open to people who have few formal qualifications, but who can demonstrate a reasonable level of literacy and numeracy, and some office experience. However, many are likely to ask for four or five GCSEs (A to C), including English and Maths, or equivalent. Higher level or more specialised roles may require GCE A-levels or equivalent, or perhaps a degree or a vocational or professional qualification.

SALARIES

r administrative assistants and officers range from over £25,000 a year, although in the civil service they are slightly higher at around £15,000 to £30,000 a year. Those with management responsibilities usually fetch around £20,000 to £60,000 a year, depending on the employer and level of seniority. The average Civil Service Fast Streamer salary is £24,500, rising to around £39,000 with experience. An environmental health practitioner can earn from around £25,000 to over £60,000 a year. Human resources professionals can earn from around £22,000 to over £50,000 a year, depending on the level of qualification and responsibility within the organisation.

Secretaries' salaries range from around £8,300 to £20,000 or more. For a personal assistant (PA), they can range from £15,000 to £30,000 or more, depending on seniority and responsibility.

SECTOR SKILLS COUNCILS (SSCs)

The SSC for central government is Government Skills.

For the voluntary sector, there is www.voluntaryskills.com and the UK Workforce Hub website.

Certain other organisations are not SSCs, but they may also help.

For voluntary organisations, there is the Scottish Council for Voluntary Organisations (SCVO) and the Wales Council for Voluntary Action (WCVA).

For local government, there is SkillsPlus UK and the Improvement and Development Agency (IDeA).

The Chartered Institute of Purchasing & Supply (CIPS), the Council for Administration (CfA) and the Management Standards Centre (MSC) may also be useful.

Engineering, construction, manufacturing and production

The occupations

The industry employs people with a variety of skill levels. They include operatives, skilled craftspeople, technicians and professionals, such as civil engineers and surveyors. They are involved in all aspects of construction, including planning, design, surveying, project management, building and fitting, inspection, renovation, and repair and maintenance.

Engineers may be involved in the research and development, design, manufacturing and production of the machinery, products and systems of everyday life; for example, cars, hospital equipment, computers, drilling rigs and communication systems. This big range means that there are many branches of engineering – marine, chemical, manufacturing to name but three.

If you are a female wannabe engineer, you may be interested in the campaign organised by Women into Science, Engineering and Construction (WISE) to encourage more women into this male dominated field. See *Useful contacts* for details.

Manufacturing industry is constantly changing as it meets the challenge of tough competition from overseas markets, where labour costs are often cheaper. People with a range of skill levels are employed, including operatives, who carry out routine but vital roles, skilled craftspeople, technicians and technologists.

Industries such as shipbuilding, textiles and motor vehicle manufacture have declined, while other industries, such as biotechnology, aerospace and pharmaceuticals, are growing. The expanding industries tend to require more highly skilled workers. Manufacturing also includes occupations in other sectors in this chapter including professional engineers, designers, scientists and creative craft workers.

Skill check

»   The ability to find solutions to challenging problems.

»   A practical approach.

»   Good communication skills.

»   A good technical knowledge of the particular industry.

» Operatives and craftspeople need practical hand skills for using tools and machinery.

» Technicians and those working at professional level require scientific understanding, as well as an ability in information technology (IT) and maths.

» Some jobs, such as that of an architect, demand creative skills, and higher level occupations usually call for management ability.

» People working outdoors on site should be physically fit.

ENTRY QUALIFICATIONS

It is possible to enter at almost any level and work through to senior positions using a combination of experience and qualifications acquired along the way. Some occupations do not require entry qualifications. Some need GCSE grades (A to C/1 to 3) or equivalent, while others require a BTEC/SQA qualification or a degree. For craft and technician occupations it may be possible to enter as an apprentice if you have GCSEs or a vocational equivalent. At higher levels you may require a degree or postgraduate degree in the specialist engineering subject.

SAMPLE SALARIES

Here are some examples of annual earnings in the construction trades:

» Bricklayers – £16,000 to £25,000.

» Carpenters and joiners – around £12,500 to £21,000.

» Glaziers – £14,000 to £40,000.

» Tilers – £18,000 to £40,000.

» Plumbers – £18,000 to £30,000 a year.

» Building technicians – £14,000 to £30,000.

» Decorators – £12,000 to £25,000.

» Plasterers – £16,000 to £25,000.

Sometimes, you may see reports in the press reporting earnings at higher rates. Some of this is exaggerated, but in parts of the UK or abroad, where demand exceeds supply, then it may be possible to earn more.

A construction manager would be able to ask for a salary of around £35,000 to £40,000. If you do not want to get your hands dirty, architects can command high salaries of more than £50,000, once they have gained a few years' experience. Architects' salaries may range from around £25,000 a year up to £100,000 or more for partners and directors.

Graduate civil engineers earn between £18,000 and £20,000, but they can progress to more senior jobs with salaries above £60,000 a year. A quantity surveyor is paid at around £35,000 to £45,000, although £50,000 or more is not unusual.

Electronics assemblers' salaries may range from around £10,000 to £20,000 a year. Engineering maintenance fitters earn from around £9,000 for apprentices, up to £32,000 for experienced fitters. Motor vehicle technicians earn from around £10,500 for a new trainee, up to £20,000 or more a year. Welders' salaries range from around £7,500 for apprentices, to £40,000 for highly skilled specialists.

Clothing pattern cutters/graders may range from £10,000 to more than £25,000 a year. For tailors and dressmakers, salaries may range from around £10,000 a year for new trainees and can reach £40,000 a year. Glassmakers range from around £8,300 to £20,000 a year. Leather craft workers start at around £9,000 a year and might exceed £20,000. Sheet metal workers may range from around £14,000 to £25,600 a year.

SECTOR SKILLS COUNCILS (SSCs)

The SSC for chemicals and pharmaceuticals, nuclear, oil and gas, petroleum and polymers is Cogent.

For property, housing, cleaning services and facilities management, it is Asset Skills.

For construction, it is Construction Skills.

For building services and engineering, it is SummitSkills.

For process and manufacturing in building products, coatings, glass, printing, extractive and mineral processing industries, it is Proskills UK.

For fashion and textiles, it is Skillfast-UK.

For food and drink manufacturing and processing, it is Improve Ltd.

Catering, hospitality, personal care, leisure, sport and tourism

The occupations

These industries are wide ranging and in some cases they feature prominently in the media.

Catering and hospitality occupations range from catering supervisors sourcing food, to chefs preparing food, waiting and bar staff serving food and drink, and front office customer service for assisting guests and housekeeping behind the scenes. Personal services include hair and beauty care, as well as cleaning and funeral services. The leisure, sport and tourism industries offer occupations including leisure centre work, coaching and instructing, professional sport, entertainment and gambling, travel and tourism.

Skill check

» A friendly and polite disposition.

» A commitment to providing a high quality of customer care and an enjoyment of dealing with the public.

» Stamina.

» The ability to work well in a team.

» Organisational skills, and a methodical and responsible approach to work.

» Staff at management level also need good organisational and problem-solving skills.

» Some occupations call for a high degree of physical fitness.

» Some occupations require good business skills.

» A professional sportsperson needs to have an exceptionally high level of skill and be totally dedicated to his sport.

ENTRY QUALIFICATIONS

There are occupations for people with a wide range of qualifications, from GCSEs or equivalent through to degrees. Entrants to hotel management usually have a Higher National Certificate (HNC) or a Higher National Diploma (HND), or a degree or postgraduate qualification. There are many relevant courses to help you prepare for entry to the industry at all levels.

SAMPLE SALARIES

Some people working in these areas become celebrities and really big earners. They get all the publicity, but, in fact, most salaries come nowhere near these levels. Salaries for chefs range from around £8,000 up to £50,000 or more. Starting salaries range from around £9,000 a year for a bar person to £30,000 or more for a bar manager. Salaries range from around £10,000 to £14,000 a year, but waiting staff are often paid by the hour. Tips from customers usually boost their income. Hotel receptionists' salaries may range from around £10,000 a year up to around £30,000, depending on the size of the hotel.

Beauty therapists earn around £12,000 basic, with the opportunity to earn commission to bump up the pay to around £15,000. A make-up artist is usually employed on a freelance basis, so earnings will be erratic. A typical income would be around £25,000.

A starting salary for a fashion designer is more like £12,000 to £14,000.

Hairdressers' salaries start from around £8,000 a year, but a senior stylist at a well-known salon could earn as much as £40,000. Tips can boost their income. Some may also take on private clients outside the salon.

Salaries for leisure centre assistants may range from around £10,000 to £14,500 a year, although this can rise to around £40,000 for managerial posts. A personal trainer at a big gym can get £30,000. Experienced yoga teachers can ask for around £40 an hour.

SECTOR SKILLS COUNCILS (SSCs)

The SSC for hospitality, leisure, travel and tourism industries is People 1st.

For sport and recreation, health and fitness, the outdoors, playwork and the caravan industry, it is SkillsActive.

The Institute of Customer Service (ICS) and HABIA, for health and beauty, may also be useful, although they are not SSCs.

Information technology (IT)

The occupations

The dramatic and sustained growth of IT continues to bring about big changes in the working environment. Most organisations, large and small, national and international, rely almost entirely on their computer systems. Moreover, the internet has seen great advances in e-commerce, database-driven websites and wireless fidelity ('WiFi') networking.

Over one million people work in IT. Occupations range from the highly technical, such as software developers, computer games designers or technical support, to those requiring good business awareness, such as systems analysts, database administrators or web authors. Occupations, such as interactive media designers or web developers, provide work in this sector for those with high levels of creativity and possibly a design background.

Skill check

» The ability to work well in a team.

» In many cases, good verbal and writing skills.

» Good technical knowledge, which can be more specialist depending on the nature of the job.

» The ability to solve complex problems in a logical manner.

» A broad knowledge of internet technologies.

ENTRY QUALIFICATIONS

There are many ways into IT, and it is possible to get a job with very different levels of educational qualifications. Some go in with a degree in IT; others may have an unrelated degree, a higher national diploma (HND) or BTEC national qualification, A-levels or equivalent, and in some cases GCSE grades or equivalent.

SAMPLE SALARIES

If you work on an IT helpdesk, you can earn around £15,000 to £20,000. Some employees get paid by the hour, typically between £12 and £15. If you acquire some extra skills and experience, you can become a technical consultant and pull in around £40,000. A software developer could command a higher salary, somewhere in the region of £45,000. Technical architects get even more, at £60,000 plus.

Strong demand for website designers, particularly in the media, has pushed up salaries to between £30,000 and £40,000. A telecoms engineer can also earn around £40,000.

SECTOR SKILLS COUNCILS (SSCs)

The SSC for IT and telecommunications, and the lead body for contact centres on behalf of the Skills for Business network, is e-skills UK.

Design, arts and crafts

The occupations

People who work in this sector use their creative and original ideas to affect the usefulness and appearance of almost everything we see and use in our daily lives.

Designers work on products ranging from clothes to cars, kitchen appliances, magazines and mobile phones, making sure that they are visually attractive, functional and, where possible, environmentally friendly. Artists produce paintings, sculpture and other pieces that adorn homes and public spaces. Craftspeople, such as engravers, picture framers and model makers, produce products using traditional techniques or innovative ideas and materials.

Employers include design companies and product manufacturers, ranging from large organisations to very small businesses. Competition for occupations is intense. About half of the workers in the design, arts and crafts sector are self-employed, and they may have to have more than one job to bolster their income.

Skill check

» Creativity.

» An eye for shape and colour.

» Good spatial awareness.

» Computer skills are essential for most design work.

» Drawing ability and practical skills are often useful.

» Craft workers need to be good at working with their hands. People who are self-employed also need business skills.

ENTRY QUALIFICATIONS

There are job opportunities at every level. Some entrants have few formal qualifications, but there is strong competition for occupations in this sector and many enter with specific art and design qualifications. There are many relevant design, art and craft courses, ranging from GCSE grades or equivalent, to those leading to degrees and postgraduate qualifications. Employers and college admission tutors also usually expect to see a portfolio of work.

SAMPLE SALARIES

The earnings of a fine artist or painter will vary enormously from person to person, and may depend a lot on commissions. Costume designers' salaries range from around £14,000 a year to £40,000 or more, but again most jobs are on a freelance basis rather than a set salary. Exhibition designers earn £18,000 to £60,000. Goldsmiths and silversmiths fetch around £10,000 to over £25,000. Salaries for employed illustrators working full time may range from around £14,000 to £40,000 a year. Self-employed illustrators are paid for each project or illustration. Signwriters and sign makers range from around £10,000, up to £30,000 or more for those with experience and managerial responsibilities.

SECTOR SKILLS COUNCILS (SSCs)

The SSC for advertising, crafts, cultural heritage, design, music, performing, literary and visual arts is Creative & Cultural Skills.

For fashion and textiles, it is Skillfast-UK.

For broadcasting, film, video, interactive media and photo imaging, it is Skillset.

Education and training

The occupations

Those who work in education and training give a wide range of people of all ages and backgrounds the opportunities to learn and develop throughout their lives. Many of those in education have a professional role as a teacher, lecturer or trainer. Additional roles, such as inspectors and assessors, are concerned with ensuring that quality standards are met in schools and in work-based learning. This sector also includes support staff, who usually work directly with pupils and students, and administrative staff who make sure that education and training institutions run smoothly.

Skill check

» For most occupations in this sector it is important to enjoy working with people.

» Spoken and written communication skills.

» A thorough knowledge of specific subjects is often essential.

» Motivational skills and the ability to give constructive criticism are important in teaching and training.

» Good organisational skills are relevant to many jobs.

ENTRY QUALIFICATIONS

You usually need a degree or postgraduate qualification to teach in schools or lecture in a college or university. Training instructors usually need a qualification related to their area of work. Experience in the subject area is more important than qualifications for some occupations in this sector, such as a learning mentor. Some occupations need a special qualification (e.g. a nursery nurse).

SAMPLE SALARIES

The minimum you would earn as a qualified teacher in England and Wales is £20,133. If you progress up the career ladder and take on extra responsibilities and training, you could earn as much as £53,000. A head teacher is looking at a salary of £35,000 at the very least. A head teacher at a big secondary school could earn as much as £98,000. A university lecturer might get between £28,000 and £38,000. A professor would earn around £50,000, or upwards of £70,000 for a dean. If you are a teaching assistant, however, you can expect around £14,000.

SECTOR SKILLS COUNCILS (SSCs)

The SSC for community learning and development, further education, higher education, libraries, archives and information services, work-based learning and development is Lifelong Learning UK.

TEACHING ENGLISH ABROAD

If you would like to learn, earn and have the opportunity to live abroad, you may want to consider taking a qualification in teaching English to foreign nationals, commonly referred to as TEFL (Teaching English as a Foreign Language).

There are many courses advertised, some part time, some online, some running over a few days. However, a certificate from a full-time course is your best chance of securing work and, providing your other credentials are up to scratch, it will fulfil most private language schools' requirements. Doing a Cambridge CELTA (Certificate in English Language Teaching to Adults) or Trinity Certificate TESOL (Teaching English as a Second Language) maximises your options, although there are some equivalent courses.

You can book through Cactus Teachers, which is a TEFL course admissions service. Also, look at the CELTA Course Survey on the Prospects website and the huge TEFL portal, TEFL.net, is a good resource. The International Association of Teachers of English as a Foreign Language (IATEFL), which is an international association for English language teachers worldwide, based in the UK, may also be of use.

Environment, animals and plants

The occupations

This sector covers a wide range of occupations at all levels, from professional to skilled and semi-skilled jobs. Careers are available in farming, fishing, countryside management and conservation, landscape design and management, forestry, gardening, tree surgery and horticulture, veterinary and animal care work.

Skill check

» A strong interest in the environment, conservation, or animal or plant care.

» Physical fitness.

» Practical skills.

» Good communication skills.

» The ability to work well in a team.

» Adaptability is important for most jobs.

ENTRY QUALIFICATIONS

For many jobs, commitment, enthusiasm and the right personal skills and qualities are the main condition for entry. Others require qualifications such as an HND or degree. Sometimes, a postgraduate qualification is useful or necessary. Many employers ask for relevant work experience.

SAMPLE SALARIES

Countryside or conservation officers fetch from £14,000 to £28,000 a year or more, and countryside rangers and wardens range from around £9,000 to more than £25,000. Salaries may range from around £8,000 a year for young people starting out as dog groomers, to around £15,000 or more for the more experienced. Arboriculturists' salaries may range from around £16,000 to £35,000.

Farm workers range from £6,267 a year at age 16 to around £19,000 with experience, and they can earn more if they are carrying out supervisory duties. Those working with livestock earn a bit extra. Forest workers may earn between £11,264 and £20,704, and gamekeeper salaries may range from around £10,000 to over £16,000.

A landscape architect can earn £18,500 to £33,000 in public sector work, and the salary may be higher in private practice. RSPCA inspectors' salaries range from £15,728 for new inspectors up to £30,000 for chief inspectors.

Zoo keepers may range from the national minimum wage to around £24,000 a year. Salaries range from £20,000 for newly qualified veterinary surgeons to £65,000 or more for very experienced vets and partners in practices.

SECTOR SKILLS COUNCILS (SSCs)

The SSC for electricity, gas, waste management and water industries is Energy & Utility Skills.

For environmental and land-based industries, it is Lantra.

Financial services

The occupations

This sector includes banking, insurance, pensions, accountancy and financial management. Occupations in this sector include customer-facing operations, such as banking, insurance broking, financial planning and investment banking. There are also central operations and back office jobs, such as fund management, credit and stock market trading, accountancy, insurance underwriting and loss adjusting.

Skill check

» The ability to work well in a team.

» The ability to be self-motivated and energetic.

» The ability to understand and interpret financial data.

» Good communication skills.

» An interest in financial and business affairs.

ENTRY QUALIFICATIONS

There is usually more than one route into most jobs. Some positions require a relevant degree. Vocational qualifications in business administration and IT can help secure occupations in banks and building societies. Many highly paid occupations in the City of London are held by young people with energy and skills developed mainly by experience.

SAMPLE SALARIES

Customer service staff earn around £12,000 a year. Those working in management positions in banks may earn from around £19,500 at first, up to £100,000 a year at senior levels. Financial management can be more lucrative for those who are successful. Earnings of over £100,000 are possible. The cut and thrust of fund management does not suit everyone, but you can still make decent money from the more traditional professions. A newly qualified accountant can expect to earn around £25,000, and maybe even closer to £35,000 in London. If you stick with it, you could be taking home upwards of £100,000 as a senior accountant or finance director.

The typical salary for a financial adviser or mortgage broker starts at around £25,000, but a successful adviser could fetch more than £75,000 including commission.

In insurance, salaries range from around £20,000 to £35,000 for trainee brokers, rising to £82,500 or more for experienced account directors. Underwriters earn from around £13,000 to £28,000 for trainees, to up to around £95,000 for senior class underwriters. Loss adjusters' salaries start at £15,000 and can rise to £40,000 or more.

SECTOR SKILLS COUNCILS (SSCs)

The SSC for the financial services industry is the Financial Services Skills Council (FSSC).

The Accountancy Occupational Standards Group (AOSG) may also be useful, although it is not an SSC.

Healthcare

The occupations

There is a wide range of occupations within the healthcare sector, including doctors and dentists, allied practitioners such as nursing staff, health visitors, physiotherapists, dieticians and radiographers, as well as complementary therapists. The sector also includes scientists working in the prevention and treatment of illness, together with health administrators, managers and other support workers.

Skill check

» Strong communication skills.

» The ability to work on your own initiative.

» The ability to work well in a team.

» A genuine concern for the well-being of patients.

» Analytical or scientific ability is essential for a number of jobs.

» A technical knowledge of the subject area (to a very high level if you are a medical practitioner).

ENTRY QUALIFICATIONS

There are opportunities at all entry levels. Some occupations do not require formal qualifications. A number of others need GCSEs (A to C/1 to 3) or equivalent, while medical professions, such as doctors, demand a degree or postgraduate qualification and a lot of supervised practical experience before an individual is considered to be fully qualified.

SAMPLE SALARIES

A new contract negotiated with the government a few years ago has pushed up the average GP's earnings to £100,000. Earnings may be topped up with extra responsibilities. A nurse's minimum starting salary is £19,000, rising to £24,800. A paramedic could expect to earn a similar amount.

Junior doctors start on around £20,000, although they can top up their earnings depending on the hours and type of work. If they rise to be consultants in an NHS hospital, they could expect a basic salary of around £70,000 to £94,000 a year. With additional payments, such as clinical excellence awards, they can earn over £160,000. Once they begin specialist training, surgeons can earn a basic salary of between £29,000 and £44,000 a year. They may be eligible for additional banding supplements.

Hospital support staffs are paid less. For porters in the National Health Service (NHS), basic pay is around £10,200 a year, although in supervisory positions they may earn £11,000 or more. Cleaners will usually earn just around the minimum wage. Health Service Managers range from around £20,000 a year for new graduate entrants up to £100,000 a year or more for some chief executives.

Salaries range from around £22,886 a year for newly qualified health visitors to around £36,400 for team managers.

As for chiropractors, salaries range from around £20,000 to over £70,000 a year. Dispensing opticians range from £14,000 to £80,000. Dietitians in the NHS may start at around £19,166 a year, and their earnings can rise as high as £34,416 where they have management roles.

NHS employees can boost their income by working in the private sector. The average NHS dentist with his own practice earned just over £100,000 in 2004/05. But more than half that income (52 per cent) was from private patients.

SECTOR SKILLS COUNCILS (SSCs)

The SSC for the health sector across the UK is Skills for Health.

Languages, information and culture

The occupations

Work in this area involves organising and providing information, and understanding and interpreting history and culture. Occupations include language interpreters and translators, librarians, archaeologists, information professionals, and museum or art gallery curators.

Skill check

» Excellent communication skills are vital with most occupations.

» Organisational skills.

» Research skills.

» Patience and attention to detail are often important.

» An interest in culture and heritage.

» Some occupations require specific technical skills (e.g. in languages) or practical skills, such as those needed in conservation work.

ENTRY QUALIFICATIONS

While many careers in this sector require specific qualifications at degree and postgraduate level, there may be some job opportunities open to people with no formal qualifications. However, as this is a highly competitive sector, qualifications such as GCSE grades or equivalent and GCE A-levels or equivalent may be an advantage.

SAMPLE SALARIES

Librarians start at between £18,000 and £22,000 a year and can reach £50,000 or more for those with management responsibilities. With curators, new entrants may start on around £15,500 and rise to £30,000 or more if they reach senior level. Earnings range from around £17,000 (sometimes less) for newly qualified translators, up to around £50,000 a year. The same is true for interpreters, although they can reach £60,000 with experience, where they are employed by international organisations. Salaries for archaeologists may range from around £13,500 to £30,000 a year.

Marketing, advertising, media, print and publishing

The occupations

Getting messages seen and heard by defined target markets is the aim of people working in marketing, public relations and advertising. Most occupations in this sector require a team approach to conduct research, develop ideas and create campaigns that communicate specific messages. They include brand management, advertising, sales and marketing, and public relations.

Working in media, print and publishing involves creating products that inform and entertain people. Administrative, craft, technical and professional opportunities are available in the printed, broadcast or internet media, including production, back room work, writing and presentation.

Skill check

» Strong communication skills.

» The ability to work well under pressure and meet deadlines.

» Excellent people skills.

» Creative skills.

» Enthusiasm.

» The ability to work within a larger team.

» Self-motivation.

» Self-confidence.

» Strong IT skills.

» Employers that specialise in promoting a particular industry sector usually require people with knowledge of that sector.

ENTRY QUALIFICATIONS

There are no set entry requirements, but competition for jobs means that many entrants, even for junior positions, have an HND or degree (or maybe a foundation degree). Candidates with relevant work experience may be at an advantage. Over two-thirds of media professionals are graduates, and many graduates apply for junior positions to gain work experience and make useful contacts. Applicants in these fields need to be persistent and committed to succeed. Relevant work experience, which may be unpaid, can be a vital step to finding paid employment. There are opportunities in printing for entrants at every level.

SAMPLE SALARIES

Everyone wants a job in the media these days, but it is not all glamour. In fact, much of it is relatively low paid. If you want to work in magazines and newspapers, salaries vary enormously, and you will not get as much working on a regional newspaper as a national. A reporter on a trade journal could expect to earn between £15,000 and £20,000.

However, a feature writer on a woman's magazine could take home double that amount. The editor of a media website could be looking at around £30,000, depending on the site's profile. If you became editor of a national newspaper, you could earn upwards of £300,000.

Most of the jobs in TV earn pretty average salaries. A runner for a TV station gets around £10,000. An editor would earn at least £25,000 and a producer can earn £50,000 upwards. Trainee researchers may earn around £8,000 a year. Experienced or specialist researchers earn up to £30,000, or from £150 to £400 a day freelancing.

A copy editor earns from £13,000 to around £19,000 a year depending on experience. A local newspaper editor may earn around £16,000 to £25,000 a year. Experienced editors and commissioning editors can earn up to £40,000. Editors working on national titles may earn over £100,000 a year.

A career in press relations or advertising can be financially worthwhile. The starting salary at WPP, one of the biggest advertising agencies, is £20,000. An account director could earn upwards of £40,000. An advertising salesperson would earn a basic wage of between £25,000 and £35,000, but the commission is usually uncapped. Salaries for press officers start at around £25,000, but a corporate communications manager could earn between £80,000 and £100,000.

SECTOR SKILLS COUNCILS (SSCs)

The SSC for advertising, crafts, cultural heritage, design, music, performing, literary and visual arts is Creative & Cultural Skills.

For broadcasting, film, video, interactive media and photo imaging, it is Skillset.

The Marketing and Sales Standards Setting Body (MSSSB), the Publishing Skills Group, the National Council for the Training of Journalists (NCTJ) and the Newspaper Society may also be useful, although they are not SSCs.

Performing arts

The occupations

Performing arts include those who make their living as actors, musicians, singers, dancers and DJs. However, there are many more people working away from the spotlight, making sure performances run smoothly, as well as promoting artists and productions. Opportunities in this area include directing theatre performances, choreography, design, and backstage occupations in stage management and organisation.

Skill check

» Creative talent as a performer in the chosen field.

» Determination to succeed despite knock backs.

» The ability to cope with rejection.

» Self-motivation.

» Strong self-confidence.

» Experience, either paid or unpaid in the chosen field; for example, in helping in school or college productions, or local amateur theatre groups, local workshops, events or festivals.

» Back room staff may not require all of the above, but they still need good organisational and people skills.

ENTRY QUALIFICATIONS

Nearly all professional performers enter the industry after training at drama or dance school, or at university. Many colleges offer a BTEC National Diploma in Performing Arts, while a range of routes is available to people wanting to work in technical or design jobs. Some start at the bottom and work their way up within the industry, learning on the job and building up experience, while many work towards relevant higher education qualifications, such as HNDs and degrees, or take vocational training in specialist areas.

SAMPLE SALARIES

Although the performing arts is a thriving industry with a high profile, it is also very competitive. Even the most successful and experienced people can find it hard to make a full-time living. There is a big pay gap between a jobbing artist and a megastar. A ballet dancer or opera singer can ask for a minimum wage of around £300 a week, according to rates negotiated by the Equity union. A West End performer could expect £367 for eight gruelling performances a week. A stunt performer ranges from around £12,000 to £25,000 a year. Stagehands fetch £12,000 to £30,000 or more.

Many people find they need to do some other part-time work to supplement their income. Equity, the actors' union, estimated that nearly half of those working in the UK performance industry earn less than £6,000 from the profession and most spend more time working outside of the industry than within it.

Musicians' pay is similarly varied. Many orchestral musicians are freelance, but the Birmingham Symphony Orchestra takes on full-time players and pays them between £26,000 and £34,000 a year. With some experience, a DJ's income is likely to be around £50 to £300 a session. A few top DJs may earn around £100,000 a year.

SECTOR SKILLS COUNCILS (SSCs)

The SSC for advertising, crafts, cultural heritage, design, music, performing, literary and visual arts is Creative & Cultural Skills.

Retail sales and customer services

The occupations

The retail sales and customer services sector offers a wide range of goods and services to customers. Retail sales staff deal directly with customers. Customer services staff may work behind a counter or in a call centre or contact centre or showroom, and are seen as essential in the constant drive to increase sales. Wholesale staff work in such organisations as builders' merchants and vehicle parts operations.

Skill check

» The ability to be friendly and helpful.

» The confidence to handle complaints in a fair but firm manner.

» In most jobs, the ability to be able to work well in a team and enjoy working with people.

» IT skills.

» Skills in handling money and finance are often necessary.

» The ability to work within a larger team.

» Managers, shop owners and other professionals need organisational and people management skills.

ENTRY QUALIFICATIONS

Many occupations in this sector do not require educational qualifications, but some employers may ask for qualifications ranging from GCSE grades to GCE A-levels, degrees or equivalent qualifications. Retail courses are available in colleges and universities throughout the country.

SAMPLE SALARIES

Checkout assistants earn around £5.55 an hour if they are over 18. Further up the food chain, a supermarket area manager earns between £38,000 and £54,000.

A buyer for a retail store can expect to start at around £25,000, but it depends on the size of the store and the reputation of the brand. Personal shoppers' starting salaries are around £16,000 to £22,000 a year. With experience, this can rise to around £30,000 or more. Butchers' salaries range from around £10,000 to £25,000 a year, and a newsagents' salary is around £12,000 to £40,000. Salaries may range from around £8,000 to £40,000 in retail jewellery. Wine merchants range from £10,500 a year at first, to around £30,000 or more with experience. Antique dealers range from £12,000 a year to £50,000.

SECTOR SKILLS COUNCILS (SSCs)

The SSC for the retail motor industry is Automotive Skills.

For retail, it is Skillsmart Retail.

The Small Firms Enterprise and Development Initiative (SFEDI) may also be useful, although it is not an SSC.

Research and development

The occupations

Scientists, mathematicians and statisticians use observation, experimentation and research to make discoveries, add to our knowledge and solve problems related to almost every aspect of our lives. They are employed in a wide range of occupations in many industries, including research and development, scientific analysis, education, the media and administration. Careers are mainly at technician and professional levels, and most people in this sector specialise in a particular field (e.g. in ecology or forensic science).

Skill check

» Researchers need to have a methodical and accurate approach to their work and be self-disciplined when they are analysing data to solve problems.

» A high level of technical knowledge of the subject area is required.

» Communication skills are important for sharing information with colleagues and customers.

» Scientists must also pay attention to health and safety regulations.

ENTRY QUALIFICATIONS

Entry is usually with a relevant degree, and often a postgraduate qualification. Some occupations require work experience as well. It is also possible to work as a technician or assistant, for which the entry requirements are usually GCSE grades (A to C/1 to 3) or equivalent.

SAMPLE SALARIES

Research scientists range from around £20,000 to over £60,000 a year. In the NHS, biochemists earn from £21,000 to £86,000, or more. Salaries range from around £18,500 to £53,000 a year for statisticians in the Government Statistical Service (GSS). Salaries in the private sector tend to be higher. Physicists' salaries range from around £18,000 to over £65,000 for senior medical physicists. Marine biologists earn from £17,000 to £60,000 a year. Mathematicians' salaries vary widely, but may range from around £24,000 to over £60,000. Salaries for geologists range from around £17,500 to over £50,000 a year. Laboratory technicians are at £11,000 to £40,000 a year.

SECTOR SKILLS COUNCILS (SSCs)

The SSC for science, engineering and manufacturing technologies is SEMTA.

The Association of the British Pharmaceutical Industry (ABPI) and the Association for Ceramic Training and Development (ACTD) may also be useful, although they are not SSCs.

The security and Armed Forces

The occupations

This sector includes people employed in a range of occupations in combat and support roles (Army, Navy and Royal Air Force), as well as police, prison, fire and rescue services staff, such as officers, instructors, crime and forensic investigators, and firefighters. Also included here is the private security industry, such as close protection officers, private investigators and security officers.

Skill check

»   Common sense.

»   Self-confidence.

- » Physical fitness.
- » Communication skills.
- » Observation skills.
- » The ability to read situations accurately.
- » Quick thinking.
- » The ability to work well within a team.
- » With some occupations, leadership qualities.

ENTRY QUALIFICATIONS

Entry and training requirements depend on the occupation and the level of entry. For instance, it is possible to join the Armed Forces in a junior rank with no educational qualifications, whereas a candidate for officer selection needs at least two GCE A-levels or equivalent before starting military training.

Police officers begin their careers at a police training centre and have to pass a two-year training probationary period. For some areas of work, a professional qualification is needed.

Skills gained in the Armed Forces and police are highly valued by commercial and public sector employers. Many transfer into private security or specialist jobs, utilising their military and police knowledge.

SAMPLE SALARIES

The starting salary in the Army is £14,000 to £23,000. If you move up the ranks to become a Warrant Officer, you could be earning £34,000.

The starting salary in the Royal Air Force is around £15,000, unless you are a commissioned officer and you can then expect at least £26,000. The Royal Navy pays sailors £14,000, but a colonel can earn upwards of £75,000. A trainee firefighter can take home around £20,000. If you rise up through the ranks, you can expect to get £50,000 or more as a divisional officer.

Police pay varies by force, but you could earn £30,000 after two years' training in the Metropolitan Police. A Met Superintendent can look forward to at least £53,000 a year. HM Prison Service pays its officers £18,000 to £27,000. A senior governor can expect to earn around £75,000. A traffic warden and similar jobs collect £11,000 to £17,000 a year.

Customs officers earn between £20,000 and £40,000, depending on their level of experience and training.

SECTOR SKILLS COUNCILS (SSCs)

The SSC for policing and law enforcement, youth justice, custodial care, community justice, the Court Service, prosecution service and forensic science is Skills for Justice.

For other security occupations, Skills for Security (SfS) may also be useful, although it is not an SSC.

Legal, advice and social work services

The occupations

This sector covers those concerned with providing information, advice and support to others. Roles are carried out by solicitors, advice workers and other staff and professionals. They may be concerned with court work, advising and assisting clients on particular topics such as welfare benefits, debt, divorce, employment law, housing, Wills, conveyancing, or supporting other legal professionals, or organising practical support for those in difficulties. Some of the support available is to help people face emotional difficulties and challenges. This is mostly carried out by counsellors and therapists. Care workers provide practical support with day-to-day living.

Skill check

»   Excellent communication skills, in both speech and writing.

» An eye for detail.

» Discretion and the appreciation of confidentiality.

» The ability to relate to people without being judgemental.

» The ability to work under pressure and meet deadlines.

» The ability to problem solve and use initiative.

» Good organisational skills and a methodical approach.

» Observational skills.

» A good knowledge of the area of law.

» Supervisors and managers also need leadership and decision-making skills.

» In many cases a genuine desire to help a person facing difficulties or someone who is in distress.

» In many cases a commitment to providing a high quality of customer care and an enjoyment of dealing with the public.

» In some cases (e.g. care workers), practical skills.

ENTRY QUALIFICATIONS

Where the work is carried out by a solicitor or social worker a degree and specialist professional qualification would be required. However, other advice and support workers are recruited more on the basis of their suitability for the role than any qualifications they may have. Training is provided in house. Previous relevant experience, either paid or voluntary, is desirable. Junior posts in legal practices and social work departments are filled by experienced administrative staff with qualifications such as GCSEs or the equivalent. A few occupations are open only to qualified barristers or solicitors.

SAMPLE SALARIES

The basic starting salary for a trainee solicitor is £14,200 a year. A partner in a large firm could earn over £100,000 a year. Salaries for legal executives may range from around £14,000 to over £50,000. Salaries for advice workers vary between employers, but they usually fall between £16,000 and £24,000, depending on the level of specialist knowledge they require. Barristers earn around £10,000 a year during pupillage (although they have no earnings at this stage in Scotland). This rises to as much as £260,000 or more for a very experienced barrister with a reputation for success.

Social workers earn at least £19,800 a year when newly qualified, to around £31,000 a year at senior level. For newly qualified counsellors, salaries begin at £15,000 a year to £37,000 or more for experienced counsellors with management responsibilities. Counselling psychologists can earn up to £70,000 or more. Care workers earn from £9,000 to £20,000.

SECTOR SKILLS COUNCILS (SSCs)

The SSC for social care, children, early years and young people's workforces in the UK is Skills for Care & Development.

The site for adult social care for England is Skills for Care.

The site for children's services (including social care) for England is the Children's Workforce Development Council (CWDC).

There is also the Care Council for Wales, the Scottish Social Services Council (SSSC) and the Northern Ireland Social Care Council.

The SSC for policing and law enforcement, youth justice, custodial care, community justice, the Court Service, prosecution service and forensic science is Skills for Justice.

ENTO may also be useful, although it is not an SSC. It is an organisation responsible for developing people in areas such as recruitment; advice, guidance and advocacy; mediation; occupational health and safety; personnel; assessment and verification; and trade unions (officers and learning representatives).

Transport and logistics

The occupations

This sector covers the range of occupations concerned with the movement of people and products. It includes those who work in shipping, and as air pilots or air crew, train crew, bus drivers, cab drivers, postal workers and couriers, together with support staff such as safety officials, maintenance workers, warehouse workers, customer service personnel and air traffic control.

Skill check

» Concentration and a mature attitude (especially for those operating transport or other machinery).

» Good communication and customer service skills.

» Good organisational skills and a methodical approach.

» The ability to use technology.

» Many occupations require people who can anticipate difficult situations and remain calm in a crisis.

» With some occupations, such as a pilot, you must be good at Maths and Physics.

ENTRY QUALIFICATIONS

These will depend on the occupation and the skill level required; for example, an airline pilot would need an Airline Transport Pilot Licence (ATPL). Entrants need at least three GCSE grades (A to C/1 to 3) or the equivalent in English, Maths and Science or the equivalent, or a pass in Maths and Physics tests. They must also pass a full medical examination. Other occupations may require GCSE grades or equivalent, or in some cases no formal qualifications on the basis that the training will be provided in house.

Occupations involving driving and operating machinery may have age restrictions, although the SSC, Skills for Logistics, operates a Young Drivers Scheme.

SAMPLE SALARIES

A member of an airline cabin crew would earn around £12,000 as a new recruit, rising to between £14,000 and £18,000 with experience. Salaries for senior crew can be up to £22,000 a year. Pilots earn around £16,500 a year to over £100,000 for some jet aircraft captains. Air traffic controller salaries may range from £10,000 to £19,000 for trainees, rising to £85,000 for some at a senior level.

Salaries for railway train drivers range from around £11,000 to £30,000 a year, and £10,000 to £23,000 for conductors. Rail track maintenance workers earn from around £12,000 to £20,000 a year before overtime payments.

Bus drivers typically earn between £10,200 and £20,000, depending on their experience. Long distance truck drivers can earn up to £35,000. Lift truck operators earn £12,000 to £20,000 a year. Postal delivery staff are on £13,000 to £18,000.

Taxi and minicab drivers range from around £11,000 a year to around £30,000. Income largely depends on the number of hours worked. Road transport managers' salaries range from around £15,000 to more than £50,000 a year.

SECTOR SKILLS COUNCILS (SSCs)

The SSC for passenger transport is GoSkills.

For freight logistics and the wholesaling industry, it is Skills for Logistics.

The Maritime Skills Alliance and the Merchant Navy Training Board (MNTB) may also be useful, although they are not SSCs.

Chapter 10

Getting a pay rise or promotion

Negotiating a salary increase

If you undergo further learning, you will improve your job prospects and increase your earnings. This will occur because you will have raised your sights in terms of the jobs to apply for, and you will be better qualified to do them. As a result of gaining a qualification, you may even be eligible to apply for a particular job for the first time.

However, you may also be in a better position to negotiate a pay rise. Here are a few tips on how you can do this.

There is no 'proper' or standard way to ask for a raise or salary increase. It is not something that people are trained to do, and little is written about it. People use various approaches. They may write to their employer, or talk to their boss informally. They may complain to their colleagues and hope that the boss happens to hear, or they may drop hints to test the water. They may ask the boss politely or demand a pay rise from him firmly. They may even go over the boss's head, or maybe even threaten to resign, secure another job offer, or simply hand in their notice.

Largely, people do not look before they leap. They are often under pressure, and they feel uncomfortable and stressed asking, so they fail to plan and control the situation, which makes achieving anything difficult. Simple planning and keeping control makes a big difference.

Here are some tips:

» **Decide on the format**

If you feel that you are not being paid enough or you have been overlooked for promotion, you can make a formal grievance. Your employer is legally obliged to consider this and respond. However, whether you want to formally complain in this way depends on your attitude to your employer. If relations are amicable, then you may want to raise the issue of your pay in a positive manner, as an application rather than a grievance. Salary negotiations are best carried out respectfully and kept in perspective, if possible.

» **Find out the correct channels**

Different types of employers respond to requests for a pay rise or promotion in different ways, depending on their policies and culture. Some, especially those in the public sector and the larger private sector companies, will refer you to set policies and protocols. For example, salary reviews may only take place at particular times in the year, or they may only be related to performance. There may be a staff handbook containing such information. Other employers – especially small ones – will have more ad hoc arrangements, but even then, there will usually be a named person who deals with such requests. If you fail to apply correctly, you will irritate people and it will not help your case.

» **Keep your boss informed**

It is normally good practice to let your immediate boss know of your position, so talk to him first. Do not go to senior managers or the human resources (HR) department over his head. Always keep your boss informed, because his opinion will usually be sought before your employer considers improving your job and remuneration package. You need your boss's support.

» **Job evaluation**

Your employer may have a policy of having fixed salary grades. In this case you are only likely to succeed in achieving a pay rise if you can argue that your job should be upgraded. To deal with this, your employer may have a job evaluation scheme. This is a method of determining the relative worth of a job to the business. You would need to compare what you are actually asked to do by your employer with the criteria set out in the scheme. The HR department may carry out a job evaluation on your job.

» **Seek support**

It may be advisable to seek support or perhaps expert representation with your application, especially if there is a procedure, such as a job evaluation, to follow. Your trade union or professional association would do this for you if you are a member. If you are not, a work colleague or friend may give you an opportunity to talk things through so that you can prepare your case.

» **Ask for extra work and responsibility**

A positive approach is to ask for extra work and responsibility and link this to an application for a pay rise; if not immediately, then in the future. Employers respond better to this rather than an employee asking for more pay for doing the same job.

» **Performance-related bonus**

Discuss with your employer how you can improve your performance and contribution to the organisation, based on standards or output greater than current or expected levels, in a way that will enable grading and pay improvement. This, again, should be received positively by the employer because you are offering something in return, and you are not simply asking for more money, which most people tend to do.

» **Secure the job offer first**

A common time to negotiate a pay rise is at the time of appointment to a job. It is important to be sure that your new employer recognises just how vital your contribution will be, so you will have to come across very well at interview. You probably will not help your chances if you try to ask for more pay before you have been offered the job.

» **Reflect on your motives**

Ask yourself honestly why you want or need a salary increase. You may feel undervalued. You may be genuinely underpaid. Are you being fair and realistic? Stepping back and taking a truly objective view is so important. Put yourself in your employer's shoes. How would the company see the situation?

» **Know your worth**

Do your homework. Research typical salaries for someone with similar experience in your industry. You can also check out salaries at recruitment firms, in job adverts and on salary surveys online. Use evidence of your value to the organisation, directly linked to cost saving, profit improvement and other key performance indicators, such as customers gained, retained, problems solved, efficiencies achieved, initiatives started, your positive effect on colleagues/team members, customer feedback and the business generated. You should also find out if people with your skills are ten-a-penny or if employers are likely to fight to the death over you. No one is indispensable, but some people are less dispensable than others, and these people will always have more leverage when it comes to salary renegotiation.

» **Think about your needs**

It is also vital that you do a bit of self-reflection. If you never stop to think about what income you need, you may end up taking an offer that leaves you pinching pennies. Before interviewing, ask yourself some important questions. How much do you need to pay your basic expenses, such as rent or mortgage, groceries, utilities and car payment? What kind of salary do you (and your family, if you live with one) need to live a comfortable life that allows you to enjoy yourself? What is the lowest salary you will consider? How much do you need to be able to save for the future?

» **Stand firm**

If you are in a position to negotiate, you should never be the first to mention a figure. Obviously, this can result in a stand off, but you should be strong and also vague. Use phrases such as, 'I am sure that if I do receive an offer, it will be fair and reasonable', or 'I will consider any reasonable offer'. Do not sell yourself short. If you have to mention a figure, start high. Say 'a package in the area of...' If you want £35,000, start at £40,000. If your employer comes up with a figure first, ask yourself if it is reasonable. If it is, start looking at the rest of the package. If you do not like the offer, ask if there is room for negotiation. You could also ask if the figure includes perks. If all else fails, tell your employer that you have been offered another job for more money, but you would prefer to work with them. This may result in goodbye, so you have to be prepared to take that risk.

» **Consider other benefits**

When you receive a job offer, it is important to consider the offer in its entirety. This means paying attention to the company's medical and dental plan, holiday allowance, retirement benefits and other perks. If the company cannot meet your salary requirements, it may be able to make it up to you in other ways, such as share options or additional holiday time.

» **Move on**

Be brave. You can turn down an offer. Doing this will give you a huge ego boost and will give you mental strength. Never get suckered into accepting an underpaying job with an elaborate title or one that offers promotion opportunities. Get paid what you are worth.

It is important that you always recognise the difference between the value of the role that you perform and your value as an individual. The two are not the same. If you continually feel frustrated about your pay levels despite trying all of the techniques and ideas for achieving a pay rise, it could be that your boss or employer has simply reached the limit of the value that he can place on your role, which is different to your value as an individual. You could have a very high potential value, but if your role does not enable you to perform to your fullest extent, then your pay level will be suppressed. For example, does a professor who sweeps the street deserve a street sweeper's salary or a professor's salary?

Aside from issues of exploitation and unfairness, if you find that the gap between your expectations and your employer's salary limit is too great to bridge, then look to find or develop a role which commands a higher value, and therefore salary. You can do this with your present employer, by agreeing wider responsibilities and opportunities for you to contribute to organisational performance and profit, or with a new employer.

Following the principles in this book, focus on developing your value to the employer and the marketplace, rather than simply trying to achieve a higher reward for what you are already doing.

Going for promotion

Your new learning will hopefully benefit your promotion prospects. In going for promotion many of the tips above apply; for example, you would still need to decide on the format of your attempt and you would need to know the correct channels (e.g. promotions may only be considered at certain times in the year). Also, you would need to keep your immediate boss informed.

» **Know the mission**

Align yourself with your boss's and company's goals and values. Make your boss's priorities your priorities.

» **Understand how you will be evaluated**

Know precisely which skills, behaviours and accomplishments you will be judged on and rewarded for, and evidence them.

» **Be dependable**

Do what you say you are going to do. Better yet, under-promise and over-deliver.

» **Project positive energy**

Do not be the one to whine or criticise the boss or company direction. Be a motivator: the person everyone wants to be around.

» **Make your boss look good**

Finish your work on time and with a high level of professionalism. Bring your boss ideas that will help him and the department, and offer to take charge and implement them.

» **Own up**

Take responsibility for your mistakes by focusing on what you have learned rather than what you have done wrong. For example, 'I think this project could have been better if we had had the group's agreement early on', or 'Next time I would talk more with the customers up front'.

» **Be organised**

Plan your next day before you leave work. Rank your tasks by urgency and importance and make a point of doing at least the top two items on your list.

» **Be punctual**

Arriving for work or meetings on time (even early) shows that you are enthusiastic, dependable and that you are able to manage your life effectively.

» **Be resourceful**

Do not run to the boss with every question you have or setback you encounter. Think things through first. If you must report a problem to the boss, develop possible solutions to present to him.

» **Broaden your horizons**

Apply the tips and approaches set out in this book to show that you are keen to learn, and show how you are developing skills and pushing against the boundaries of your job role.

» **Stay informed**

Keep abreast of industry and company trends by reading trade journals and attending professional association events. Stay up to date with current trends and with technological, legal and knowledge advances in your area. Upgrade your skills and learn new ones.

» **Be courteous**

Show respect and loyalty to your boss and speak well of him to others. (At the very least, do not bad mouth him to anyone.)

» **Be flexible**

Change is inevitable. Companies need people who can adapt and go with the flow.

» **Take care of your health**

When you are run down, productivity and ambition suffer, as does your image.

» **Leave your personal life at the door**

Using your colleagues as therapists not only hurts productivity, but it damages your credibility and it is detrimental to your work relationships (even if people seem sympathetic).

» **Go beyond the call of duty**

Take on added challenges, put in extra hours, and never use the phrase 'That is not in my job description'.

» **Be a team player**

Show your boss and colleagues that you have their best interests at heart by being empathetic and offering to help out when they need it.

» **Take a break now and then**

A clear head and balanced life can give you energy and perspective.

» Look and act promotable

Do not let anyone think that you work because you have to. While you are waiting for your dream vacancy to appear, make something happen for yourself. Rather than wait to be given the new job and new responsibilities, start looking for ways to become more valuable and effective in your organisation while performing your current role. In doing so, you will almost inevitably create a promotion for yourself – in a job that you love – because you will have defined it for yourself.

The techniques here might not secure a salary increase immediately – there are usually very good reasons (such as the salaries budget or the company's trading performance) why this is not possible anyway – but these ideas will eventually bring a better reward and outcome than doing nothing, or doing something the wrong way.

Appendix

Useful contacts

Accountancy Occupational Standards Group (AOSG)

140 Aldersgate Street   Tel: 020 7397 3046
London EC1A 4HY   Email: info@aosg.org
Website: www.aosg.org

Advisory Conciliation and Arbitration Service (ACAS)

Head Office   Tel: 0845 747 4747
Brandon House   Email: equalityservices@acas.org.uk
180 Borough High Street   Website: www.acas.org.uk
London SE1 1LW

Aimhigher

Website: www.aimhigher.ac.uk

Apprenticeships

Website: www.apprenticeships.org.uk

Assessment and Qualifications Authority (AQA)

Stag Hill House   Tel: 0870 410 1041
Guildford   Email: mailbox@aqa.org.uk
Surrey GU2 7XJ   Website: www.aqa.org.uk

Asset Skills

2 The Courtyard   Tel: 0800 056 7160

48 New North Road
Exeter EX4 4EP

Website: www.assetskills.org

Association of British Correspondence Colleges (ABCC)

PO Box 17926
London SW19 3WB

Tel: 020 8544 9559
Email: info@homestudy.org.uk
Website: www.homestudy.org.uk

Association of the British Pharmaceutical Industry (ABPI)

12 Whitehall
London SW1A 2DY

Tel: 0870 890 4333
Website: www.abpi.org.uk

Association for Ceramic Training and Development (ACTD)

St James House
Webberley Lane
Longton
Stoke-on-Trent ST3 1RJ

Tel: 01782 597 016
Website: www.actd.co.uk

Association for Coaching

66 Church Road
London W7 1LB

Website: www.associationfor
coaching.com

Association of MBAs

25 Hosier Lane
London EC1A 9LQ

Tel: 020 7246 2686
Website: www.mbaworld.com

Automotive Skills

Fanshaws
Brickendon
Hertford SG13 8PQ

Tel: 01992 511 521
Email: info@automotiveskills.org.uk
Website: www.automotive
skills.org.uk

Basic Skills Agency

Commonwealth House

Tel: 020 7405 4017

1–19 New Oxford Street
London WC1A 1NU

Email: enquiries@basic-skills.co.uk
Website: www.basic-skills.co.uk

British Computer Society

1st Floor
Block D
North Star House
North Star Avenue
Swindon SN2 1FA

Tel: 0845 300 4417
Email: customerservice@
hq.bcs.org.uk
Website: www.bcs.org

British Psychological Society

St Andrews House
48 Princess Road East
Leicester LE1 7DR

Tel: 0116 254 9568
Email: enquiry@bps.org.uk
Website: www.bps.org.uk
Psychological Testing Centre
website: www.psychtesting.org.uk

Business in the Community

137 Shepherdess Walk
London N1 7RQ

Tel: 0870 600 2482
Email: information@bitc.org.uk
Website: www.bitc.org.uk

Business Link

Tel: 0845 600 9006
Website: www.businesslink.gov.uk

Cactus Teachers

Tel: 0845 130 4775
Website: www.cactusteachers.com

Care Council for Wales

South Gate House
Wood Street
Cardiff CF10 1EW

Tel: 029 2022 6257
Email: info@ccwales.org.uk
Website: www.ccwales.org.uk

Chartered Institute of Personnel and Development (CIPD)

151 The Broadway
London SW19 1JQ

Tel: 020 8612 6200
Website: www.cipd.co.uk

Chartered Institute of Purchasing & Supply (CIPS)

Easton House
Easton on the Hill
Stamford
Lincolnshire PE9 3NZ

Tel: 01780 756 777
Website: www.cips.org

Children's Workforce Development Council (CWDC)

3rd Floor
Friends Provident House
13–14 South Parade
Leeds LS1 5QS

Tel: 0113 244 6311
Email: info@cwdcouncil.org.uk
Website: www.cwdcouncil.org.uk

Citizens Advice Bureau (CAB)

Advice website: www.adviceguide.org.uk
Citizens Advice website: www.citizensadvice.org.uk (to locate a CAB)

City & Guilds

1 Giltspur Street
London EC1A 9DD

Tel: 020 7294 2800
Website: www.city-and-guilds.co.uk

The Coaching Academy

39–43 Putney High Street
London SW15 1SP

Tel: 020 8789 5676
Email: info@the-coaching-academy.com
Website: www.the-coaching-academy.com

Coaching & Mentoring Network

PO Box 5551
Newbury

Tel: 0870 733 3313
Email: annabg@coaching

Berkshire RG20 7WB
network.org.uk
Website: www.coaching
network.org.uk

Cogent

Unit 5, Mandarin Court
Centre Park
Warrington
Cheshire WA1 1GG

Tel: 01925 515 200
Website: www.cogent-ssc.com

Community Service Volunteers (CSV)

237 Pentonville Road
London N1 9NJ

Tel: 020 7278 6601
Email: information@csv.org.uk
Website: www.csv.org.uk

Connexions

Tel: 0808 001 3219
Website: www.connexions-direct.com

Construction Skills

Bircham Newton
Kings Lynn
Norfolk PE31 6RH

Tel: 01485 577 577
Email: information.centre@cskills.org
Website: www.cskills.org

Council for Administration (CfA)

6 Graphite Square
Vauxhall Walk
London SE11 5EE

Tel: 020 7091 9620
Email: info@cfa.uk.com
Website: www.cfa.uk.com

Creative & Cultural Skills

4th Floor
Lafone House
The Leathermarket
Weston Street
London SE1 3HN

Tel: 020 7015 1800
Email: info@ccskills.org.uk
Website: www.ccskills.org.uk

Department for Business, Enterprise & Regulatory Reform (BERR)

Ministerial
Correspondence Unit
1 Victoria Street
London SW1H 0ET

Tel: 020 7215 5000
Email: enquiries@berr.gsi.gov.uk
Website: www.berr.gov.uk

Department for Children, Schools and Families

Sanctuary Buildings
Great Smith Street
London SW1P 3BT

Tel: 0870 000 2288
Email: info@dcsf.gsi.gov.uk
Website: www.dfes.gov.uk

Department of Education (Northern Ireland)

Rathgael House
Balloo Road
Bangor BT19 7PR

Tel: 028 9127 9279
Email: mail@deni.gov.uk
Website: www.deni.gov.uk

Department for Education, Lifelong Learning and Skills (Wales)

Cathays Park
Cardiff CF10 3NQ

Tel: 0845 010 3300
Email: DELLSWebTeam@
wales.gsi.gov.uk
Website: new.wales.gov.uk/topics/
educationandskills/?lang=en

Department for Employment and Learning (NI)

Adelaide House
39–49 Adelaide Street
Belfast BT2 8FD

Tel: 028 9025 7777
Email: del@nics.gov.uk
Website: www.delni.gov.uk

Department of Health

Richmond House
79 Whitehall
London SW1A 2NS

Tel: 020 7210 4850
Email: dhmail@dh.gsi.gov.uk
Website: www.dh.gov.uk

Department for Work and Pensions (DWP)

Website: www.dwp.gov.uk

Direct.gov

Website: www.direct.gov.uk

Do-it.org.uk

1st Floor
50 Featherstone Street
London EC1Y 8RT

Tel: 020 7250 5700
Website: www.do-it.org.uk

Duke of Edinburgh's Award

Gulliver House
Madeira Walk
Windsor SL4 1EU

Tel: 01753 727 400
Email: info@theaward.org
Website: www.theaward.org

Edexcel

One90 High Holborn
London WC1V 7BH

Tel: 0844 576 0026 (for BTEC and NVQ enquiries)
Tel: 0844 576 0028 (for diploma enquiries)
Website: www.edexcel.org.uk

Educational Grants Advisory Service (EGAS)

501–505 Kingsland Road
London E8 4AU

Tel: 020 7254 6251
Website: www.egas-online.org.uk

Employment Tribunals Service

Tel: 0845 795 9775
Website: www.employmenttribunals.gov.uk

England & Wales

100 Southgate Street
Bury St Edmunds IP33 2AQ

Tel: 01284 762 171

Scotland

The Eagle Building   Tel: 0141 204 0730
215 Bothwell Street
Glasgow G2 7TS

Energy & Utility Skills

Friars Gate   Tel: 0845 077 9922
1011 Stratford Road   Email: enquiries@euskills.co.uk
Shirley   Website: www.euskills.co.uk
Solihull
West Midlands B90 4BN

Engineering Construction Industry Training Board (ECITB)

Blue Court   Tel: 01923 260 000
Church Lane   Email: ECITB@ecitb.org.uk
Kings Langley   Website: www.ecitb.org.uk
Herts WD4 8JP

ENTO

Kimberley House   Tel: 0116 251 7979
47 Vaughan Way   Email: info@ento.co.uk
Leicester LE1 4SG   Website: www.ento.co.uk

e-skills UK

1 Castle Lane   Tel: 020 7963 8920
London SW1E 6DR   Email: info@e-skills.com
                                  Website: www.e-skills.com

European Computer Driving Licence Foundation

3rd Floor   Tel: +353 (0)1 630 6000
Portview House   Website: www.ecdl.com
Thorncastle Street
Dublin 4
Ireland

European Mentoring & Coaching Council

Wildhill
Broadoak End
Hertford SG14 2JA

Tel: 01992 550 246
Email: enquiries@emccouncil.org
Website: www.emccouncil.org

eVolunteer.co.uk

88 Clinton Road
London E3 4QU

Tel: 020 8981 6924
Website: www.eVolunteer.co.uk

The Experience Corps

117 Waterloo Road
London SE1 8UL

Tel: 020 7921 0565
Website: www.experiencecorps.co.uk

Financial Services Skills Council (FSSC)

51 Gresham Street
London EC2V 7HQ

Tel: 0845 257 3772
Email: info@fssc.org.uk
Website: www.fssc.org.uk

Find a Life Coach

Email: info@findalifecoach.co.uk
Website: www.findalifecoach.co.uk

Floodlight

Tel: 0800 100 900
Website: www.floodlight.co.uk

Foundation Degree Forward

Lichfield Centre
The Friary
Lichfield WS13 6QG

Tel: 01543 301 150
Website: www.fdf.ac.uk

Foundation Degrees

Website: www.foundationdegree.org.uk

Foyer Federation

3rd Floor	Tel: 020 7430 2212
5–9 Hatton Wall	Email: inbox@foyer.net
London EC1N 8HX	Website: www.foyer.net/mpn

General Federation of Trade Unions (GFTU)

Central House	Tel: 020 7387 2578
Upper Woburn Place	Website: www.gftu.org.uk
London WC1H 0HY	

General Social Care Council (GSCC)

Goldings House	Tel: 020 7397 5800
2 Hay's Lane	Website: www.gscc.org.uk
London SE1 2HB	

GoSkills

Concorde House	Tel: 0121 635 5520
Trinity Park	Email: info@goskills.org
Solihull	Website: www.goskills.org
West Midlands B37 7UQ	

Government Skills SSC Secretariat

c/o Cabinet Office	Tel: 020 7276 1611
Admirality Arch	Website: www.government-
The Mall	skills.gov.uk
London SW1A 2WH	

HABIA

Oxford House	Tel: 0845 230 6080
Sixth Avenue	Email: info@habia.org
Sky Business Park	Website: www.habia.org
Robin Hood Airport	
Doncaster DN9 3GG	

Health and Safety Executive (HSE)

HSE Infoline
Caerphilly Business Park
Caerphilly CF83 3GG

Tel: 0845 345 0055
Website: www.hse.gov.uk

Higher Education and Research Opportunities (HERO)

Website: www.hero.ac.uk

Hot Courses

Website: www.hotcourses.com

ILA Scotland

PO Box 26833
Glasgow G2 9AN

Tel: 0808 100 1090
Email: enquiries@ilascotland.org.uk
Website: www.ilascotland.org.uk

Improve Ltd

Ground Floor
Providence House
2 Innovation Close
Heslington
York YO10 5ZF

Tel: 0845 644 0448
Email: info@improveltd.co.uk
Website: www.improveltd.co.uk

Improvement and Development Agency (IDeA)

Layden House
76–86 Turnmill Street
London EC1M 5LG

Tel: 020 7296 6880
Email: ihelp@idea.gov.uk
Website: www.idea.gov.uk

Institute of Customer Service (ICS)

2 Castle Court
St Peter's Street
Colchester
Essex CO1 1EW

Tel: 01206 571 716
Email: enquiries@icsmail.co.uk
Website: www.instituteofcustomer
service.com

International Association of Teachers of English as a Foreign Language (IATEFL)

Darwin College
University of Kent
Canterbury CT2 7NY

Tel: 01227 824 430
Email: generalenquiries@iatefl.org.
Website: www.iatefl.org

International Coach Federation (ICF)

248 Walsall Road
Bridgtown
Cannock
Staffordshire WS11 0JL

Tel: 0870 751 8823
Email: info@coachfederation.org.uk
Website: www.coachfederation.
org.uk

Investors in People (IIP)

7–10 Chandos Street
London W1G 9DQ

Tel: 020 7467 1900
Website: www.investorsin
people.co.uk

Jobcentre Plus

Tel: 0845 606 0234
Website: www.jobcentreplus.gov.uk

Jubilee Sailing Trust

Hazel Road
Woolston
Southampton SO19 7GB

Tel: 023 8044 9108
Email: info@jst.org.uk
Website: www.jst.org.uk

Lantra

Lantra House
Stoneleigh Park
Coventry
Warwickshire CV8 2LG

Tel: 0845 707 8007
Email: connect@lantra.co.uk
Website: www.lantra.co.uk

LCCI Examinations Board (LLCIEB)

Tel: 0870 720 2909
Website: www.lccieb.com

Learn Direct

Tel: 0800 100 900
Website: www.learndirect.co.uk

Learn Direct Business

Tel: 0800 015 0750
Website: www.learndirect-business.co.uk

Learn Direct Scotland

Tel: 0808 100 9000
Website: www.learndirectscotland.com

Learning and Skills Council (LSC)

Cheylesmore House
Quinton Road
Coventry CV1 2WT

Tel: 0870 900 6800
Email: info@lsc.gov.uk
Website: www.lsc.gov.uk

Learning and Skills Development Agency (LSDA)

Website: www.lsda.org.uk

Learning through Work

University of Derby
Kedleston Road
Derby DE22 1GB

Tel: 01332 591 698
Email: ltw@derby.ac.uk
Website: www.learningthrough
work.co.uk

Lifelong Learning

Website: www.lifelonglearning.co.uk

Lifelong Learning UK

5th Floor
St Andrew's House
18–20 St Andrew Street
London EC4A 3AY

Tel: 0870 757 7890
Email: enquiries@lifelonglearning
uk.org
Website: www.lifelonglearninguk.org

Management Standards Centre (MSC)

3rd Floor
17–18 Hayward's Place
London EC1R 0EQ

Tel: 020 7240 2826
Email: management.standards@
managers.org.uk
Website: www.management-
standards.org

Maritime Skills Alliance

1 Hillside
Beckingham LN5 0RQ

Tel: 01636 629 115
Website: www.maritimeskills.org

Marketing and Sales Standards Setting Body (MSSSB)

Moor Hall
Cookham
Berkshire SL6 9QH

Tel: 01628 427 106
Email: info@msssb.org
Website: www.msssb.org

Mentoring and Befriending Foundation

1st Floor
Charles House
Albert Street
Eccles
Manchester M30 0PW

Tel: 0161 787 8600
Email: info@mandbf.org.uk
Website: www.mandbf.org.uk

Mentoring UK

Website: www.mentoring-uk.org.uk

Merchant Navy Training Board (MNTB)

Carthusian Court
12 Carthusian Street
London EC1M 6EZ

Tel: 020 7417 2800
Email: enquiry@mntb.org.uk
Website: www.mntb.org.uk

Move On Up

Tribal Education and
Technology

Tel: 01223 478 291
Email: info@move-on.org.uk

Mitre House
Tower Street
Taunton
Somerset TA1 4BH

Website: www.move-on.org.uk

National Association for Voluntary and Community Action (NAVCA)

The Tower
2 Furnival Square
Sheffield S1 4QL

Tel: 0114 278 6636
Website: www.navca.org.uk

National Bureau for Students with Disabilities (Skill)

Chapter House
18–20 Crucifix Lane
London SE1 3JW

Tel: 020 7450 0620
Email: skill@skill.org.uk
Website: www.skill.org.uk

National Centre for Languages (CiLT)

3rd Floor
111 Westminster Bridge Road
London SE1 7HR

Tel: 020 7379 5101
Email: info@cilt.org.uk
Website: www.cilt.org.uk

National Council for the Training of Journalists (NCTJ)

The New Granary
Station Road
Newport
Saffron Walden
Essex CB11 3PL

Tel: 01799 544 014
Email: info@nctj.com
Website: www.nctj.com

National Database of Accredited Qualifications (NDAQ)

Tel: 020 7509 5556
Email: NDAQ@qca.org.uk
Website: www.accreditedqualifications.org.uk

National Extension College (NEC)

Michael Young Centre

Tel: 01223 400 200

Purbeck Road
Cambridge CB2 8HN

Email: info@nec.ac.uk
Website: www.nec.ac.uk

National Institute of Adult Continuing Education (NIACE)

Renaissance House
20 Princess Road West
Leicester LE1 6TP

Tel: 0116 204 4200
Email: enquiries@niace.org.uk
Website: www.niace.org.uk

National Open College Network (NOCN)

The Quadrant
Parkway Business Park
99 Parkway Avenue
Sheffield S9 4WG

Tel: 0114 227 0500
Email: nocn@nocn.org.uk
Website: www.nocn.org.uk

National Trust

PO Box 39
Warrington WA5 7WD

Tel: 0870 458 4000
Email: enquiries@thenational
trust.org.uk
Website: www.nationaltrust.org.uk

National Union of Students (NUS)

2nd Floor
Centro 3
Mandela Street
London NW1 0DU

Tel: 0871 221 8221
Email: nusuk@nus.org.uk
Website: www.nusonline.co.uk

Newspaper Society

St Andrew's House
18–20 St Andrew Street
London EC4A 3AY

Tel: 020 7632 7400
Email: ns@newspapersoc.org.uk
Website: www.newspapersoc.org.uk

Northern Ireland Social Care Council

7th Floor
Millennium House

Tel: 028 9041 7600
Email: info@niscc.n-i.nhs.uk

19–25 Great Victoria Street
Belfast BT2 7AQ

Website: www.niscc.info

Open College of the Arts (OCA)

Registration Department
Freepost SF10678

Tel: 0800 731 2116
Email: open.arts@ukonline.co.uk
Website: www.oca-uk.com

Open and Distance Learning Quality Council (ODLQC)

Tel: 020 7612 7090
Email: info@odlqc.org.uk
Website: www.odlqc.org.uk

Open University

PO Box 197
Milton Keynes MK7 6BJ

Tel: 0845 300 6090
Website: www.open.ac.uk

Oxford Cambridge and RSA Examinations (OCR)

Tel: 01223 553 998
Email: general.qualifications@ocr.org.uk
Website: www.ocr.org.uk

People 1st

2nd Floor
Armstrong House
38 Market Square
Uxbridge
Middlesex UB8 1LH

Tel: 0870 060 2550
Website: www.people1st.co.uk

Prince's Trust

18 Park Square East
London NW1 4LH

Tel: 020 7543 1234
Website: www.princes-trust.org.uk

Project Trust

The Hebridean Centre
Isle of Coll
Argyll PA78 6TE

Tel: 01879 230 444
Website: www.projecttrust.org.uk

Proskills UK Ltd

Centurion House
85B Milton Park
Abingdon
Oxfordshire OX14 4RY

Tel: 01235 432 032
Email: info@proskills.co.uk
Website: www.proskills.co.uk

Prospects Postgraduate Funding Guide

Graduate Prospects
Prospects House
Booth Street East
Manchester M13 9EP

Tel: 0161 277 5200
Website: www.prospects.ac.uk

Public Concern at Work

Suite 301
16 Baldwins Gardens
London EC1N 7RJ

Tel: 020 7404 6609
Email: whistle@pcaw.co.uk
Website: www.pcaw.demon.co.uk

Publishing Skills Group

South House
The Street
Clapham
Worthing
West Sussex BN13 3UU

Tel: 01903 871 686
Email: info@publishingskills.org.uk
Website: www.publishing
skills.org.uk

Qualifications and Curriculum Authority (QCA)

Customer Relations
83 Piccadilly
London W1J 8QA

Tel: 020 7509 5555
Email: info@qca.org.uk
Website: www.qca.org.uk

Quality Assurance Agency for Higher Education (QAA)

Southgate House
Southgate Street
Gloucester GL1 1UB

Tel: 01452 557 000
Email: comms@qaa.ac.uk
Website: www.qaa.ac.uk

Raleigh International

3rd Floor
207 Waterloo Road
London SE1 8XD

Tel: 020 7183 1270
Email: info@raleigh.org.uk
Website: www.raleigh.org.uk

Reach

Website: www.volwork.org.uk

Residential Training Unit

Government Office for the
North East
Citygate
Gallowgate
Newcastle upon Tyne NE1 4WH

Tel: 0191 202 3579
Email: rtu@gone.gsi.gov.uk
Website: www.go-ne.gov.uk/gone/
educationandskills/skills/rtu

Retired and Senior Volunteer Programme (RSVP)

237 Pentonville Road
London N1 9NJ

Tel: 020 7643 1385
Email: rsvpinfo@csv.org.uk
Website: www.csv-rsvp.org.uk

Royal National Institute of Blind People (RNIB)

105 Judd Street
London WC1H 9NE

Tel: 020 7388 1266
Website: www.rnib.org.uk

Ruskin College

Walton Street
Oxford OX1 2HE

Tel: 01865 554 331
Email: enquiries@ruskin.ac.uk
Website: www.ruskin.ac.uk

Samaritans

PO Box 9090
Stirling FK8 2SA

Tel: 0845 790 9090
Email: jo@samaritans.org
Website: www.samaritans.org

Scottish Council for Voluntary Organisations (SCVO)

Mansfield Traquair Centre
15 Mansfield Place
Edinburgh EH3 6BB

Tel: 0800 169 0022
Website: www.scvo.org.uk

Scottish Executive

Tel: 08457 741 741
Email: ceu@scotland.gsi.gov.uk
Website: www.scotland.gov.uk

Scottish Qualifications Authority (SQA)

The Optima Building
58 Robertson Street
Glasgow G2 8DQ

Tel: 0845 279 1000
Email: customer@sqa.org.uk
Website: www.sqa.org.uk

Scottish Social Services Council (SSSC)

Compass House
11 Riverside Drive
Dundee DD1 4NY

Tel: 0845 603 0891
Email: enquiries@sssc.uk.com
Website: www.sssc.uk.com

Sector Skills Council for Science, Engineering and Manufacturing Technologies (SEMTA)

14 Upton Road
Watford
Hertfordshire WD18 0JT

Tel: 01923 238 441
Website: www.semta.org.uk

Sector Skills Development Agency (SSDA)

3 Callflex Business Park
Golden Smithies Lane

Tel: 01709 765 444
Email: reception@ssda.org.uk

Wath-upon-Dearne
South Yorkshire S63 7ER

Website: www.ssda.org.uk

Skillfast-UK

Richmond House
Lawnswood Business Park
Redvers Close
Leeds LS16 6RD

Tel: 0113 2399 600
Email: enquiries@skillfast-uk.org
Website: www.skillfast-uk.org

Skills for Care (formerly Topss England)

Albion Court
5 Albion Place
Leeds LS1 6JL

Tel: 0113 245 1716
Email: info@skillsforcare.org.uk
Website: www.skillsforcare.org.uk

Skills for Care & Development

4th Floor
Albion Court
5 Albion Place
Leeds LS1 6JL

Tel: 0113 241 1251
Email: sscinfo@skillsforcareand
development.org.uk
Website: www.skillsforcareand
development.org.uk

Skills for Health

2nd Floor
Goldsmiths House
Broad Plain
Bristol BS2 0JP

Tel: 0117 922 1155
Email: office@skillsforhealth.org.uk
Website: www.skillsforhealth.org.uk

Skills for Justice

Centre Court
Atlas Way
Sheffield S4 7QQ

Tel: 0114 261 1499
Website: www.skillsforjustice.com

Skills for Logistics

14 Warren Yard

Tel: 01908 313 360

Warren Farm Office Village
Milton Keynes MK12 5NW

Email: info@skillsforlogistics.org
Website: www.skillsforlogistics.org

Skills for Security (SfS)

Security House
Barbourne Road
Worcester WR1 1RS

Tel: 0845 075 0111
Email: info@skillsforsecurity.org.uk
Website: www.skillsfor
security.org.uk

SkillsActive

Castlewood House
77–91 New Oxford Street
London WC1A 1PX

Tel: 020 7632 2000
Email: skills@skillsactive.com
Website: www.skillsactive.com

Skillset

Focus Point
21 Caledonian Road
London N1 9GB

Tel: 020 7713 9800
Email: info@skillset.org
Website: www.skillset.org

Skillsmart Retail Ltd (The Sector Skills Council for Retail)

4th Floor
93 Newman Street
London W1T 3EZ

Tel: 0800 093 5001
Email: contactus@skillsmart
retail.com
Website: www.skillsmartretail.com

SkillsPlus UK

Website: www.skillsplus.gov.uk

Small Firms Enterprise and Development Initiative (SFEDI)

Business Incubation Centre
Durham Way South
Aycliffe Industrial Park
County Durham DL5 6XP

Tel: 01325 328 306
Website: www.sfedi.co.uk

Social Work Careers

Tel: 0845 604 6404
Website: www.socialworkcareers.co.uk

Springboard

Website: www.springboard.hobsons.co.uk

Student Awards Agency for Scotland (SAAS)

Gyleview House
3 Redheughs Rigg
Edinburgh EH12 9HH

Tel: 0845 111 1711
Website: www.student-support-saas.gov.uk

Student Loans Company

100 Bothwell Street
Glasgow G2 7JD

Tel: 0845 607 7577
Website: www.slc.co.uk

Student Volunteering England

Website: www.studentvol.org.uk

SummitSkills (The Sector Skills Council for Building Services Engineering)

Vega House
Opal Drive
Fox Milne
Milton Keynes MK15 0DF

Tel: 01908 303 960
Email: enquiries@summitskills.org.uk
Website: www.summitskills.org.uk

TEFL.net

23 King Street
Cambridge CB1 1AH

Website: www.tefl.net

TimeBank

2nd Floor
Downstream Building
1 London Bridge SE1 9BG

Tel: 0845 456 1668
Website: www.timebank.org.uk

Training and Development Agency for Schools

151 Buckingham
Palace Road
London SW1W 9SZ

Tel: 0845 600 0991
Website: www.tda.gov.uk

UK National Reference Point for Vocational Qualifications

Oriel House
Oriel Road
Cheltenham
Gloucestershire GL50 1XP

Tel: 870 990 4088
Email: info@uknrp.org.uk
Website: www.uknrp.org.uk

UK Workforce Hub (Voluntary and Community Sector)

Regents Wharf
8 All Saints Street
London N1 9RL

Tel: 0800 652 5737
Email: help@ukworkforce
hub.org.uk
Website: www.ukworkforce
hub.org.uk

Universities and Colleges Admissions Service (UCAS)

Customer Service Unit
PO Box 28
Cheltenham GL52 3LZ

Tel: 0871 468 0468
Email: enquiries@ucas.ac.uk
Website: www.ucas.com

University for Industry (Ufi)

Dearing House
1 Young Street
Sheffield S1 4UP

Tel: 0114 291 5000
Website: www.ufi.com

V

5th Floor
Dean Bradley House
52 Horseferry Road
London SW1P 2AF

Tel: 020 7960 7000
Website: www.wearev.com
Website: www.vinspired.com (for
16 to 25 year-olds)

Voluntary Service Overseas (VSO)

317 Putney Bridge Road
London SW15 2PN

Tel: 020 8780 7200
Website: www.vso.org.uk

voluntaryskills.com

Website: www.voluntaryskills.com

Volunteer Development Agency (for Northern Ireland)

129 Ormeau Road
Belfast BT7 1SH

Tel: 028 9023 6100
Email: info@volunteering-ni.org
Website: www.volunteering-ni.org

Volunteer Development Scotland

Stirling Enterprise Park
Stirling FK7 7RP

Tel: 01786 479 593
Email: vds@vds.org.uk
Website: www.vds.org.uk

Volunteering England

Regents Wharf
8 All Saints Street
London N1 9RL

Tel: 0845 305 6979
Email: volunteering@volunteering
england.org
Website: www.volunteering.org.uk

Volunteering Wales

Website: www.volunteering-wales.net

Wales Council for Voluntary Action (WCVA)

Baltic House
Mount Stuart Square
Cardiff Bay
Cardiff CF10 5FH

Tel: 029 2043 1700
Email: enquiries@wcva.org.uk
Website: www.wcva.org.uk

Women into Science, Engineering and Construction (WISE)

2nd Floor
Weston House
246 High Holborn
London WC1V 7EX

Tel: 020 3206 0408
Email: info@wisecampaign.org.uk
Website: www.wisecampaign.org.uk

Youth Action

Crest House
7 Highfield Road
Edgbaston
Birmingham B15 3ED

Tel: 0121 455 9732
Email: info@youth-action.org.uk
Website: www.youth-action.org.uk

Index

The index categorises the Introduction and all chapters. Entries are terms in full unless these are known primarily in their abbreviated form.